Table of Contents

Preface

Let's face it. Life is stressful. For most of us, a significant part of life's stress is linked to finances. Sometimes, it's just plain hard to keep it together and save at the same time. A lot of us live paycheck to paycheck, barely scraping by and wondering how long we can keep our heads above water. I wrote this book to show you that life doesn't have to be that way. You can manage your expenses, save money and even enjoy the things that make life fun—and you may be surprised to discover that it really isn't as hard as you thought it might be.

Among the many life lessons that I've learned over the years, one critical lesson that tops the list is that "life is life." The unexpected should be expected!

One of the ways that I've managed to survive the unexpected is by developing systems to manage life's routine responsibilities so that I'm prepared to efficiently and effectively manage life's chaos, while still saving money and achieving financial freedom.

For the past three decades—notice that I said decades instead of thirty years—I've practiced zero-based budgeting to manage my household finances. Trust me when I tell you that zero-based budgeting has been the cornerstone of the management of my personal finances.

While I understand that zero-based budgeting won't work for everyone, it does work. I'm a Type A personality, so I find great comfort in covering all of the bases, which allows me to save and take advantage of the sweetness of life without risking that comfort.

Here's my story—it can be your story, too.

Every family has THAT aunt. The aunt that has been unofficially elected family matriarch without the benefit of a formal vote. In my family, THAT aunt was my Aunt Ellen.

As children, all the cousins hated visiting Aunt Ellen and Uncle Mac, because their house was over-filed with "collectibles." At each visit, after we were presented to them so they could see how much we'd grown, our parents always instructed us to be seated on the patio where we were not allowed to move—for the entire visit (never mind that a visit to Aunt Ellen and Uncle Mac's could last for several hours), for fear that we would break something.

Aunt Ellen must have agreed with them because she made a habit of "checking on us" a number of times during those visits.

My Aunt Ellen was a very elegant woman. She was always perfectly coiffed and perfectly dressed. No outfit was complete without pearls, pearls and more pearls. She loved jewelry. Lots and lots of jewelry. When I was sixteen, she gifted me with a "diamond" ring that I still cherish to this day.

As she required, until the day he died my uncle treated her as though she was Cleopatra reincarnate. He also demanded that the rest of the world do the same. Not doing so was guaranteed to result in his displeasure.

While the rest of the world called him Mac, she always affectionately called him McNeil (my eldest son's middle name). At the time of his death, my Aunt Ellen and my Uncle Mac were married for 73 years.

Part of her job as the family matriarch was gifting my cousins and I with nicknames. Nicknames she felt foreshadowed our futures.

The nickname bestowed upon me was "Grandma." She explained that she nicknamed me "Grandma" because I was an "old soul." My "grandma-ness" has manifested itself in a number of ways throughout my life. As always, Aunt Ellen was right.

As a "Grandma," even as a young child, I was always much more of an observer than a participant. I preferred to observe people's actions and decide who they were based on what I observed, rather than on what they said.

While I worked throughout high school, it was on my first real job that I observed the payday rituals of the women in my office. On payday, they would rush to the bank to cash their paychecks, purchase new clothes and treat themselves to a special lunch in celebration of payday. By the middle of the very next week these same women were borrowing lunch money. That is all but one.

With my "Grandma" in full effect, I noticed that one of the women—Miss Barbara Kent—resisted joining in on this ritual. She didn't rush to the bank to cash her check. Barbara didn't purchase new clothes. She didn't treat herself to a special payday lunch. More important to me, she wasn't borrowing lunch money the very next week. In fact, most times it was Barbara that the other women were asking to lend them lunch money. She did not oblige them. She didn't believe in lending money unless she knew with 99.99% certainty that she would be repaid. Needless to say, she was not very popular. I, however, was fascinated with her.

Instead Barbara spent her lunch hour in the breakroom performing her own payday ritual. After a couple of weeks of observing her versus the other women, I decided to join her in the breakroom.

For a couple of months, I slyly (or so I thought), watched her perform her payday ritual using index cards, ink pens, white out and rubber bands.

Still fascinated with her, I finally mustered up the courage to ask her what she was doing. Her response? "Meet me in the breakroom next payday and I'll show you."

Now in the spirit of full disclosure, not only did I notice that Barbara didn't participate in the community payday ritual, I also noticed that as a single mother, she was well-dressed, owned a two-family home, drove a brand new car, and supported both her daughter and her son through college.

I suspected that her lifestyle had something to do with those index cards and I was right.

The following payday, I met her in the breakroom equipped with my "supplies," which made her laugh. She smiled and said that she was aware that I had been watching her. I wasn't as sly as I thought I was.

I was an eager student. As Barbara explained her budget process—which at the time, I didn't realize was zero-based budgeting—I listened intently. I asked questions. I took notes. I asked more questions. I took more notes. Then I went to work.

While it took a while for me to work out the kinks, zero-based budgeting has guided me through a wedding (paid for in cash), purchasing a home (with a healthy down payment), maternity leave for two children (six months for each), divorce, the financial support of a terminally ill parent, and college tuition (for both my sons). In other words, through life. I'm a firm believer that you can't manage chaos unless you manage calm. Zero-based budgeting allows you to manage the calm and survive through the chaos.

Now, this is not to say that I haven't struggled financially, because I have. But there is no doubt that the management of my finances using the principles of zero-based budgeting has served me well.

With gratitude, this book is dedicated to the fascinating Ms. Barbara Kent and to my elegant Aunt Ellen.

"Money is only a tool. It will take you wherever you wish, but it will not replace you as the driver."

Ayn Rand

1

At Zero

What Is Zero-Based Budgeting?

Sound money management all starts with a budget. For many people, though, the word "budget" is a negative. Nothing could be further from the truth: A budget is simply a spending plan. The type of budgeting we have come to know, however, emphasizes where your money went—after the fact—instead of telling you beforehand where your money should go.

Know Yourself (And Your Spending Habits)

Certainly, tracking your spending has value. It makes you more conscious of where you are "bleeding" so you can be moved—or shocked—into stanching the flow. But budgeting doesn't stop there. Being aware is just half the battle; putting that awareness into action gets you much closer to your financial goals. That is why a written plan is essential, because it will easily tell you at a glance whether you are on track or not.

Unfortunately, like incomes, all budgets are not created equal. Some are good at letting you know how much you have left to spend for the rest of the month, while others are better at painting the big picture without connecting it to the specifics.

Zero-Based Budgeting: A Better Type of Spending Plan?

There's a specific type of spending plan that tells you not only where your money goes, but also forces you to allocate your resources carefully, both on paper and in reality. It's called zero-based budgeting: Which means that your total income minus your total expenses should be equal to zero.

At its very core, zero-based budgeting is all about "giving every dollar a job," whether that job is to pay your mortgage, cut down your debt, or create an emergency cushion, it's all up to you as long as every dollar gets to work. In theory and in practice (as most adopters of this budgeting plan have come to realize), by telling every dollar where to go, you should not have any money left over to waste when you use zero-based budgeting.

Many financial experts believe this type of budgeting works better than other systems, because it allows you to reflect on paper the reality of your spending, lets you connect one month to the next, and forces you to give surplus money a job after all the expense categories are satisfied.

With zero-based budgeting, you will be able to gain total control over the dynamics of your spending from month to month so you can easily redirect any windfall to a category, prepare for anticipated expenses in the coming months by creating a cushion this month, address unexpected expenses, by allowing you to adjust other categories so your expenses do not go beyond your income (and lead you back to where you started).

Setting Up a Zero-Based Budget

Total your income sources in a month. This is simple if you're an employee. For entrepreneurs and freelancers, simply take the average of your monthly income for the past 3 to 4 months.

Categorize your monthly expenses – include everything – then categorize them into three types:

- Fixed expenses, such as rent, mortgage payments, etc.

- Semi-fixed expenses, such as electricity and utilities that fluctuate may vary every month.
- Variable expenses, such as entertainment spending and other regular expenses whose amount varies each month.

Assign the exact amount from your income to fixed expenses first. Next, allocate part of your income to your semi-fixed expenses (*use the average monthly amount from the past three months*). Last, budget what's left of your income to your variable expenses. The key here and what your main focus should be is to make sure that all your monthly expenses are covered by your income.

What If My Income Is Not Enough To Cover All The Expenses?

- First, identify which are necessities and disregard the non-essentials
- Discover ways to lessen your costs in your fixed costs, i.e. save on your utilities, and increase deductibles on your home or auto insurance.
- Consider launching a side hustle to make extra income.

What If My income is More Than Enough to Cover All the Expenses?

- Congratulations! You're living below your means.
- Assign any "leftover" funds to "Savings" or "Investment Budget."
- Last, allocate some of it to FUN—you deserve it!

Continue to adjust your budget until all your money has been "spent on paper." Don't stop until every cent has been assigned— which means your "Income" less your "Expenses" is equal to "Zero," (*thus the name of the system*).

- Review your budget status and progress once a week. Constantly work on how you can improve your system until your budget is working like a fine-tuned machine.

Applying Zero-Based Budgeting In Real Life

Zero-based budgeting can seem overwhelming at first, eating up what little free time you have. But once you have laid the groundwork, it gets easier to manage over time, because all you need to do is fine-tune your plan.

Using $5,500 monthly expenses, perhaps you broke it down as follows:

Mortgage	1,000
Credit Cards	1,500
Groceries	900
Utilities	300
Gas	250
Auto Loan	500
Cell Phones	100

Entertainment	450
Clothes	200
Miscellaneous	100

If this is how your monthly expenses look and the least amount of income you earn in a month is $5,000, maybe you can decide to do away with entertainment and clothes for now, reduce your groceries by a third ($300), and maybe downgrade your cellphone and Internet plan. Then whatever money you have left, you can allocate it to a cushion category until you come up with the needed $5,500 for you to be a month ahead of your expenses.

By working around the least amount of income you have at your disposal, you can redirect additional income to debt reduction, emergency cushion, or retirement savings.

Reconciling the Plan with Your Reality

As with anything that is worth doing, you have to keep practicing until you get the general concept down. It also helps to have some tricks up your sleeve to help make the process run smoother. To make zero-based budgeting work in real life, keep some of these tips in mind:

Plan for Everything

Say you have renewal of car registration coming up. Plan for it a few months ahead, and put some money toward it every month. Maybe you can label it as a deferred expense. When the bill is due, you don't have to adjust categories to accommodate this periodic expense.

Pad Your Variable Expenses

Because you can plan for everything and still come up short, inflating your variable expense will at least provide a bit of cushion when an unforeseen expense (like birthday gifts or health emergencies) sneaks up on you. Variable expenses are costs that fluctuate—gas, electricity and other utilities. You won't be caught off guard if you have overshot your variable expenses, because then you can use any leftover amount from this category to cover overages in other categories. If your variable expenses are underutilized, you can reassign them as deferred expenses so when something else comes up that hasn't been planned for, you can just draw it out against this category.

Check Your Spending Regularly

Your plan is only as good as your ability to consult it often. After all, that's what plans are for. They help keep you on track. The purpose is to alert you to any category that might go over the budget so that you will have some time left before the end of the month to adjust your spending accordingly. If you have discovered that you have overspent in one category, you will at least have the time to adjust some other categories so your expenses remain in line with your income.

Keep An Open Mind

Zero-based budgeting evolves from month to month, and unpredictability is also its downside. What you can do, however, is learn to adapt; if certain expenses look viable on paper, but impossible in real life, you can adjust them to reflect your reality so you don't feel deprived. If you have pared down your budget to the bone and you still can't make ends meet, then maybe a side job—or a lifestyle overhaul—is in order.

Zero-Based Budgeting: More Than a Financial Plan

In this respect, zero-based budgeting is not just a financial plan; it could very well be a life plan, because it forces you to look at how you live your life and the problems that will persist if you don't make changes. Zero-based budgeting requires that you identify problem areas and compels you to address them either by setting a limit you can live with, or expanding your sources of income so you can accommodate all the things you consider as your necessities.

For expenses incurred more or less often than monthly, convert the payment to a monthly amount when calculating the monthly budget. For instance, convert an auto expense that's billed every six months to a monthly amount by dividing the six-month premium by six. This money should be kept separate from your other money so it's available when the bill becomes due.

To help you with creating your personal household budget, you can find a free zero-based household budget template here.

"Too many people spend money they haven't earned to buy things they don't want to impress people they don't like."

Will Smith

2

After Zero

Better Budgeting For Life

Now, you may be thinking, "What else can there be? If I follow this advice, I'll have everything I need to create and follow a monthly budget. That should be enough, right?" Actually, while sticking with a monthly zero-based budget is a great step in the right direction, it's not the end of the road. There's a budgeting solution beyond this that makes even more sense and can take you even farther—weekly zero-based budgeting.

In this step after zero-based budgeting, you will continue to budget for your monthly utilities, housing costs, etc., the same way every month. However, you'll make a new weekly budget for your regular expenses.

Why opt for a weekly budget for these expenses? When you look at what you'll be doing in the near future, how do you break your time down? You break it down by what you're doing *this week*, not what's happening this month. Furthermore, it's much easier to manage smaller numbers over a shorter timeframe, and it allows you to work with more manageable numbers on a schedule that makes sense to you.

So how do you create these weekly budgets, and how can you make them work better for you as an extension of your monthly zero-based budget?

Using the Envelope Method to Manage Your Weekly Budget

If you spend $500 per month on groceries, in a four-week month you spend $125 per week at the grocery store. When you look at it this way, it's going to be much easier to get to the end of the month with money still in your "Groceries" envelope, because you only have to think of it on a weekly basis. How much easier is it to say, "I'm only going to spend $125 at the store over the next seven days," than to try to spread $500 over 30 or 31 days? Much, much easier.

Keep It Simple

Next, take your regular weekly budgets and simplify them down to three envelopes of expenses per week. When you're working on a monthly basis, it makes sense to have a different category or envelope for every expense, especially when you're just getting started with your new budget and you're still fine-tuning your budgeting.

Once you're ready to create and maintain weekly budgets, though, it's time to simplify things. I personally recommend having three envelopes: groceries, entertainment, and other.

Your "Groceries" envelope will obviously only be spent at the grocery store. "Entertainment" includes hobbies, eating out, going to the movies, etc. "Other" will include gas and other incidentals that you regularly spend money on. With this simplified weekly budget, you can spend money on some fun stuff without breaking the bank or ruining your zero-based monthly budget. It gives you some freedom with your spending without letting you backslide into your old careless spending habits.

Allow Room For Human Error

The reason I particularly like the "Other" envelope is that it gives me a little bit of margin for error. If I'm expecting company over for dinner, I might end up spending $175 or $200 at the grocery store one week. With this budget system, that doesn't mean my family has to live on ramen noodles for the rest of the month. It just means I'll use $50-75 from that week's "Other" envelope.

Now, I know that I told you earlier not to "borrow" from different envelopes, but with a weekly budget built into your monthly zero-based budget, you specifically have room to breathe in case you don't account for everything you need at the grocery store.

Keep Tracking Your Spending

Finally, while it's okay to use your "Other" envelope's cash for groceries or even for a little bit of entertainment (as long as you're not going over your overall budget for the week), it's important to keep tracking your spending. Whether you do this with your envelopes or a mobile app, keep track of how much you have left in each weekly budget category at the end of each week, as well as where you stand on your monthly budget. The more you track your spending, the more conscious you'll be of where you're spending it and where all of your income is going.

The more conscious you are of where your money goes, the more likely you'll be to stop before you buy that $8 cup of coffee or that $200 coat (when you already have a perfectly good coat in your closet). Your money can do a lot more for you than you might think, and with the combination of a weekly and monthly budget, you can make it stretch in ways you never thought possible.

"If you can, you will quickly find that the greatest rate of return you will earn is on your own personal spending. Being a smart shopper is the first step to getting rich."

Mark Cuban

3

Beyond Zero

After you've "zeroed out" and can see the benefit of zero-based budgeting, it's time to take it to the next level. Just be mindful that zero-based budgeting is an ever-evolving discipline that must be tweaked every so often in order to be successful.

In today's economic climate, most financial advisors recommend that we have 6-8 months of emergency savings available to us to manage the unexpected.

One of the easiest ways to build an emergency fund is by "finding" money by reviewing both fixed and variable expenses for cost-saving opportunities and earmark those savings for building your fund.

For example, in my household one of the hardest areas to manage is food shopping. I'm addicted to the latest flavor of Cheerios, to say nothing of pumpkin muffins during Thanksgiving season. To manage this passion, I've had to go so far as using a home-delivery service for my weekly grocery shopping (my service accepts both store and manufacturers coupons, which helps lower delivery costs) to keep me out of the aisles!

Following are cost-cutting tips in areas that have challenged me that I hope you will find useful.

Hack Your W-4

Getting a big tax return in April feels good, but what about the rest of the year? Wouldn't it be great to get more money in each paycheck so that you have your cash when you earn it?

When you complete your W-4 for your job, your employer will withhold a certain percentage of your check for taxes. The amount they withhold is based on your withholding allowance, which is a number derived from the number of allowances and exemptions that you declare.

If you don't have any allowances or exemptions, then you'll have the maximum amount withheld for your tax bracket. If you add allowances and/or exemptions, then you'll have less withheld and you'll get a smaller tax return the following April. The goal here should be to withhold as little as possible without owing the IRS a lot of money come tax season. You can do this by using the work-sheet on the W-4 form or by getting some help from an accountant.

When you go this route, you will have more monthly income that you can add to your budget, and you'll have cash when you need it instead of living on less money throughout the year and waiting on your tax return every April.

To help you determine your allowances, you can find an excellent withholding calculator from Turbo Tax here.

Keep It Moving ...

One of the key principles of zero-based budgeting is that the process is never-ending. You must continue your search to cut costs to allocate savings to building your emergency fund, or to pay down debt. One of my favorite methods of achieving that is by finding incremental savings.

So what exactly does that mean? Incremental savings simply refers to the reduction or elimination of the cost of a recurring expense. Typically, incremental savings require only a one-time action up front or a substitution of one action for another so that there's no change in your time investment. If you find a way to trim your energy bill, then that's incremental savings. If you find a way to trim your grocery bill that's repeatable, then that's incremental savings.

The benefits of incremental savings are obvious. It means smaller bills, so that means you're going to have more money left behind for other things in life. That usually means lower stress in life and far fewer money worries. More important, because it costs very little time—it's just one up-front task that doesn't have to be repeated, or a substitution of tasks that doesn't add any additional time—they have very little opportunity costs associated with them. You're not going to miss out on other things because you're devoting time to these projects, because they're either one-shot things you can do in your downtime, or substitutions for the things you already do.

Here are some of my favorite incremental savings strategies. Hopefully, you're already doing most of these things. If not, you have a great avenue for easy savings.

Trim Your Energy Bill By Replacing Light Bulbs With LEDs

- Many American homes are still lit by incandescent bulbs and CFLs, each of which have their own problems. Incandescent bulbs are very cheap up front, but they have a pretty short lifespan and they gobble energy like there's no tomorrow. CFLs are better in terms of energy use and have a longer lifespan, but they take a while to warm up and are more expensive than incandescent.
- LEDs, on the other hand, light up instantly, have an incredibly long lifespan, use less energy than even CFLs do and the newer ones offer full spectrum lighting that's indistinguishable from

a normal incandescent. The only drawback is the upfront cost, but that's recouped by the fact that you won't have to replace one for many years.

- The solution is easy: as the bulbs in your home burn out, start replacing them with LED bulbs, one at a time. You'll find that before long, light bulbs become a pretty rare purchase and your energy bill will slowly decline, too.

Trim Your Energy Bill By Air Sealing Your Home

- Air sealing your home simply means looking for places where air freely flows in and out of your home when you don't want it to happen, such as through window edges, under doors, and through the attic. Doing some basic air sealing can cut down on that air transfer, meaning you keep cool air inside in the summer and warm air inside during the winter. *That* means that your air conditioning runs less in the summer and your furnace runs less in the winter, which means lower energy bills for you.
- Air sealing your home really isn't that hard, either. It's mostly just a bunch of very small home improvement projects, such as applying caulk to windows, installing a weather strip on the bottoms of doors, and adding insulation where needed (especially in the attic).

Trim Your Energy Bill by Opening Windows Instead Of Using Climate Control

During the hottest days of summer and coldest nights of winter, you're going to want to close your windows tight and turn on the air conditioning or the furnace, depending on the season. However, the reality is that most days and most seasons don't reach those extremes. Often, the temperature outside isn't incredibly different than it is inside.

During the nicer winter and summer days and most spring and fall days, consider turning off your heating or cooling system and just opening the windows. You might not have the exact temperature that you want in your home if you do this—the temperature can vary a lot when the windows are open—but it will be in a range where you'll still be comfortable and best of all, you won't be paying the energy bills for heating and cooling.

It's easy enough. Whenever the temperature outside is within 20 degrees of what you ideally want inside, turn off your air conditioner or furnace and open up some windows. You'll find that your energy bill goes down and your home still feels wonderful.

Trim Your Energy Bill By Running Ceiling Fans Correctly Based On The Season

A ceiling fan in a room can go a long way toward making it comfortable by encouraging air flow and circulating the air throughout the room. During the summer, you simply want air motion to create the cooling effect that you feel on your skin. In the winter, when you're more interested in having the warm air that collects near the ceiling, move toward the middle of the room and the floor where people can feel it. If a ceiling fan is doing its job, it enables you to turn off your furnace or air conditioning at a wider variety of temperatures, saving on your energy bill.

How do you achieve that? Ceiling fans have a little switch on them that changes the direction of the blades. Stand directly underneath the fan with the fan running. If you feel air blowing down on you, then the blades are moving in the right direction *for the summer months*. Otherwise, if you barely feel air moving at all, the blades are moving in the right direction *for the winter months*.

If the blades are moving in the wrong direction for the season, turn off the fan and flip the switch that controls the direction of the blades and you're good to go for the next six months or so.

We tend to leave the ceiling fans in our house running most of the time with the blades in the correct seasonal direction. This enables us to rarely turn on our central air or furnace, which cuts down on our energy bill overall since the fans use very little energy.

Trim Your Cable Bill By Eliminating Premium Channels That You Don't Watch

Take a look at your most recent cable or satellite bill. What packages are you subscribed to? Do you have a channel package that's much larger than the "basic" package that's offered? Do you have any premium channel packages added onto that, like HBO or Starz?

Now, ask yourself how often you actually watch those channels. Do you really watch anything on there with any frequency? Maybe you subscribe to HBO just to watch *Game of Thrones*, in which case you're paying somewhere around $180 a year just to watch one television program. Maybe you have a big extended package, but you really only watch two channels 99% of the time and they're in the most basic package.

The key here is to remember that *it's only worth paying for channels you actually watch.* It is *never* worth paying for channels that you rarely or never watch. Watching a channel for one or two hours a month does not justify an additional $10 or $15 on your cable bill.

Focus on keeping the 20% of channels that make up 80% of your viewing and drop the rest.

Trim Your Cable Bill By Shopping Around For A Better Cable Or Satellite Service

If you're not under any sort of contract for your cable or satellite service, you're a free agent. It's time to start shopping around for a better offer.

My recommendation is to do as suggested in the previous tip and figure out which channels make up 80% of your television viewing, then start examining packages from various companies which will provide those channels at the lowest possible price. Make sure that you're factoring in the "teaser" prices that companies offer, as many companies will give you a great rate for the first year of a cable contract, but the prices inflate during the second year. Average the "teaser" and regular prices in that situation.

For starters, the satellite providers (Dish Network and DirecTV) are available almost everywhere in the United States. Many towns also have a cable provider or two (Mediacom, Comcast, Time Warner or someone else) and some towns have their own local provider as well. Do your homework and compare all the options, then switch to the one that will save you a bundle each month.

Trim Your Cable Bill By Cutting the Cord

Another option for cutting your cable bill down to size is simply eliminating that bill and using over-the-air free television signals along with your Internet plan and the streaming video services that the Internet provides to give you all of the television viewing options you need.

Getting over-the-air, high-definition television signals is easy and extremely cheap if you live within 50 miles or so of a city. Just buy a digital antenna at your local electronics store or on Amazon and install it by mounting it on a wall and attaching it to your television. The internal tuner in your television will take care of the rest.

For additional programming, services like Netflix, Hulu, and Video add a ton of additional programming to your television for $10 a month (or less) via your Internet connection. Combine that with sports services like MLB.tv and you can easily replace most of what you enjoy from cable for a much lower price.

Trim Your Credit Card Bills By Negotiating Lower Interest Rates

If you carry a balance on your credit card and face a minimum monthly payment each month, you'll quickly realize that much of that monthly payment is made up of interest. Rather than repaying what you borrow, a lot of that check you send in just goes to the company, with only a small fraction actually going to reduce your debt.

If you want to lower your monthly payment, the most effective thing you can do (besides paying it off, of course), is to negotiate a lower rate. Simply call up your credit card company and tell them that you're struggling to cover the bills and may not be able to do so in the future. Ask for a reduction in interest rate and, if the person you're talking to can't do that, ask to speak to that person's supervisor and ask *that* person for a lower rate. Remain calm and positive throughout the call.

It's worth noting here that sometimes credit card issuers will close your account (leaving you still with a bill) or reduce your credit limit if you do this, so be aware that this is a potential outcome. Don't negotiate your rate on a card that you *need*.

Trim Your Credit Card Bills By Using Balance Transfers

Another approach for reducing your credit card bills is to transfer high-interest balances to other credit cards that offer a lower interest rate. Many credit cards offer an introductory 0% interest rate on balance transfers, which means every dollar you send in directly pays off the balance.

Many credit cards offer reduced interest balance transfer offers, particularly cards that offer this as a bonus for signing up. They essentially issue a payment on your behalf to your other credit card and then add that payment amount to your new card, where that amount earns zero interest for an extended period of time.

While this doesn't mean that you can just ignore that transferred amount, as it *will* eventually have an interest rate again, you often can get away with a reduced payment here for the time being. You can also take advantage of that 0% interest rate and make larger payments to get rid of that debt completely before the interest rate comes back. In either case, you're going to wind up with lower bills, whether now or later.

Trim Your Credit Card Bills By Switching To Another Card For Primary Usage

Different cards have different features. For people who carry a balance, interest rates are a very important part of the equation. For others, the program associated with the card can make a big difference too, and can save you money in other ways.

First of all, let's look at the situation where you carry a balance from month to month. In those situations, you should rate credit

cards and, ideally, one with an introductory balance transfer program so you can move the balance from your higher interest card.

If you don't carry a balance, you may want to look at a credit card that has a better bonus that comes along with using the card. Cards offer rewards up to as high as 5% cash back or a 5% discount at specific retailers, so if you get a MasterCard or Visa associated with the retailer you shop at most frequently that can be a sweet deal.

If you're looking for a better card, you can start looking at The Simple Dollar's list of the best credit card offers we've found.

Trim Your Student Loans By Consolidating Them

Student loans can be a real burden for anyone who's freshly graduated from an institution of higher learning.

In general, there's not much benefit to consolidating federal student loans acquired after 2006, as they have a fixed interest rate. If you do consolidate them to get a longer repayment term, you'll lower your bills for the moment but you'll be in repayment for much longer, and that will cost you more money in the long run.

The real savings comes from consolidating private loans, which allows you to easily shop around among lenders to find the best deal for consolidating your private student loans. You can drastically reduce both your monthly payment and your interest rate by doing this, if this is an option that's useful for you.

Trim Your Grocery Bill By Switching To The Most Cost-Effective Grocery Store In Your Area

Most people get into a routine of shopping at the same grocery store or two all of the time and don't even consider changing it. However, it's very likely that the store you use regularly isn't actually the best store for your dollar.

I recommend trying to shop at a bunch of different stores over the course of a month or two, buying many of the staples that you usually buy at each different store—buy milk, cheese, bread, and vegetables, and so on according to what you normally buy.

Keep track of the receipts and then compare them when you're done checking out a lot of stores. The store you should be shopping at is the one that offers the best prices on the items you buy regularly. If you do this, your grocery bill will naturally shrink from here forward.

Trim Your Grocery Bill By Buying More Store Brand Items And Fewer Name Brand Items

Many people gravitate toward name brands due to familiarity, and to a smaller extent, attractive packaging. Yet when you do this, you're paying extra for advertising and for a pretty picture on the box. It has virtually no impact on what's inside the box.

My recommendation for anyone is to try out some generic or store brand versions of the items that normally fill up your grocery list. Try out things like store brand bread, store brand cereal, store brand dish soap, store brand canned tomatoes, store brand frozen vegetables, and so on.

What you'll find is that most of the time you'll not even notice a difference between the two, except that the store brand costs less, which means that you have more money left in your pocket. Try out store brands, stick with the ones that click for you, and enjoy a lower average grocery bill.

Trim Your Medication Bill By Trying Generic Versions Of The Medications That You Use

If you're a regular user of prescription medications and your medical insurance isn't topnotch, it's very likely that there's a significant price difference for you between the regular version and the generic version of the medication. If the generic version can save you a bundle, it's worth considering.

Your first step is to talk to your doctor about it. Will the generic medication take care of your problem? Many generics are identical to the name brand medication, but in some cases, they're not. Your doctor will know whether a generic version is right for you.

If your doctor approves and writes a prescription, go to your pharmacy and give it a try! If it works exactly the same, your prescription expenses will drop through the floor, which can make an enormous difference in your monthly expenses.

Trim Your Banking Bill By Switching To A Bank Without Fees For The Services That You Use

If you use a bank that charges you for having a checking account or constantly dings you with ATM fees, you need a new bank. Those are expenses you really don't need in your life, especially since there are many banks that *don't* charge such fees and competition is heavier than ever in the banking space.

You should look at the multitude of banks and credit unions in your area to see what they offer in terms of interest rates and fees for the services that you use. You should also compare those offerings with what's available in terms of online only banks, such as Ally Bank and Smarty Pig.

If you switch to a bank that eliminates your banking fees and earns you a little more interest, you'll see your expenses drop naturally and also see a bit more earnings as well without any real effort from you.

Trim Your Life Insurance Bill By Switching To A Term Policy (With A Few Caveats)

If you have a fairly recently established universal or whole life insurance policy (within the last year or two), it's probably going to make short-term and long-term financial sense to cancel that policy and replace it with a term policy.

The reality is that the "investment" portion of many life insurance policies isn't that good until you've dumped money in it for years and years. If you've reached the five-year mark or so on such a policy, it actually can become a fairly solid investment, but in the early years, it's really not very good and you never really fully earn back those years.

If you don't have a life insurance policy and have any dependents, you should strongly consider getting one, and I recommend a term policy for the biggest benefit you can afford.

Trim Your Cell Phone Bill By Shopping Around For A Better Plan

Much as with your cable bill, if you're in a situation where you're not tied to a cell contract, it makes a *ton* of financial sense for you to shop around and look at other providers, because they often offer great deals for new customers who switch to them (and sometimes you can get the "new customer" deals from your current provider if you mention that you're considering switching).

Check out the wide array of cell phone providers in your area, including both the big ones like Verizon and Sprint and smaller ones like US Cellular. Figure out which company offers the best deal for you as a new customer on the services that you actually use and then make the big switch.

For the most part, switching cell companies is pretty painless. You keep your same number and the only real difference is that you're paying a much lower bill to a different provider.

Trim Your Cell Phone Bill by Considering Pay-As-You-Go Providers, Especially If You're A Relatively Low Intensity User

Many pay-as-you-go companies (like my personal favorite, Ting) actually offer a very good deal for people who aren't heavy users of cell phones.

Usually, such pay-as-you-go companies have a la carte offerings where you can pick and choose which services you want. Do you want unlimited texting for a certain dollar amount each month? Or what about a capped number of texts for a lower amount?

Unlimited voice, or a certain number of minutes? How much data each month?

Take a hard look at what you actually use. You'll probably find that you use far less than you're actually paying for with your provider. If you're already using a low-end plan, take a hard look at what pay-as-you-go companies can give you. You can save a lot of money each month.

Trim Your Membership Bills By Downgrading Or Eliminating Services That You Rarely Use

Do you really use Netflix all that often? What about your gym membership? What about any other online services that you subscribe to, whether it's a software subscription or anything else?

My rule of thumb is this: if I'm not using a subscription service enough to drop the price down to a dollar or two per hour of usage, it's not worth my money. Anything that costs me more than that per hour better be giving me a *lot* of benefit.

Walk through your credit card and bank statements and figure out what services you're paying for each month. If those services aren't providing significant value for you, cancel them! Those savings can really add up!

Trim Your Entertainment Bills By Renting Entertainment First Instead Of Buying It

This one's real easy.

If you buy a lot of books, start going to the library first instead of the bookstore. If you buy a lot of movies, start going to the library first and, if that doesn't work, check out Redbox or other video rental kiosks and, if that doesn't work, rent them online from sites like Amazon.

The truth is that most books we buy never get read multiple times, and most movies we buy never get watched more than once. Don't buy either until you're sure it's going to see multiple viewings.

If you take a serious approach to trimming your spending, incremental savings can help a *ton* in terms of lowering your expenses without adding even more time commitments to your life. If you can take action on even five of these twenty tips, you're going to be saving real money on all of your regular expenses from here on out.

Good luck!

Grocery Budgeting Made Easy: Tips On How to Get Started and Make a Lasting Change

American households spend around 13-15% of their overall expenditures for groceries and of that percentage, 60% goes to at-home cooking, while 40% goes to eating out. So no matter how difficult it is for you to lower your budget, you can always find ways to trim it down with the right mindset and tools. When you are committed enough to make a change, you will find—and fund— ways to make it happen.

That said, your grocery budget, like your life, is only going to change if you are willing to change it. And it all starts with creating a budget and putting it in place so it becomes a habit.

The Importance of Zero-Based Grocery Budgeting

A budget is a spending plan; without a plan, you're likely to veer off the track. Without a budget, your coupon-clipping, bargain-shopping or deal-hunting may even waste you money (because you might be tempted to hunt deals for things you don't need in the first place), negating whatever savings you thought you had.

Because it's written down in black and white, a budget lets you track your spending so you'll be made more aware of where you can trim down without hurting your lifestyle. It gives you boundaries you can work with to serve your purpose, as well as freedom to live creatively within those parameters.

Setting Up A Grocery Budget You Can Live With

Once you warm up to the idea of a budget and get used to the lifestyle it affords, you may even love budgeting enough that you are inspired to increase your savings and decrease your spending. Here's how to get it started.

Compute Your Average From The Last 4-8 Weeks

The basis for your initial grocery budget depends on how much you have been spending, on average, for the last 4-8 weeks. You would want a reasonable amount you can live with comfortably, or you won't be able to stick with it for too long. The ultimate goal is to be able to whittle down your grocery costs without feeling deprived. But you need to have a budget in the first place, because it sets the tone to curb your spending.

Set Realistic Amounts

Much like diets, a budget that's too severe will make you give up early instead of sticking with it for the long haul. When you are just starting out, an impossibly low amount will discourage you from further pursuing budgeting. A budget is a spending plan; plan well, and you may even indulge in little treats here and there. It's crucial to make room for some purchases that will give you satisfaction or, just like a dieter on a lemon cleanse, you'll end up so deprived you'll blow five days' worth of your budget on a fancy meal.

Decrease Your Spending Gradually

It's impractical to expect that you'll be cutting your grocery budget in half in as short as a month. Like any good plan worth realizing, lower your budget gradually, maybe a 5% cut here and there over a period of six months to a year. Eventually, it won't hurt as much to reduce your grocery budget by 30% if you've slowly adapted to a smaller amount over a longer period. If you do go over-budget by $50, don't beat up yourself. It's just a budget, not the end of the world.

Why You Should Plan Your Meals

Setting a grocery budget lays the groundwork for wise spending come shopping time, but it's not the only thing that will help you cut your expenses gradually. Menu-planning is as important as budgeting, if only because it provides a tasty alternative to eating out.

Saves You Stress And Frustration

Last minute grocery shopping will not only leave you frazzled and frustrated, it will also make you feel guilty and a failure at budgeting. But you can get past that 5:00 p.m. dread with a list of recipes planned a week ahead. It also saves you frequent trips to the grocery store, and allows you to indulge in food your family wants to eat without unnecessarily overspending.

Saves You Time And Money

The simple act of sitting down and writing down what to eat for the week can save you significant amounts of money, frustration and guilt. It can also make a huge difference in your life given the dangers of fast food, if that's what you reach out for every time you're running late for dinner.

Of course, buying everything all at once saves you fuel too, so you're also doing your bit toward helping the environment while saving on gas money. Plus, if you already have all the ingredients to a wonderful recipe, it's a lot easier to just grit your teeth and cook the meal than it is to drive everyone to the nearest restaurant, look for parking, wait to be seated, and wait some more for the food to be served.

Your menu doesn't have to be inflexible, either. You can tweak it as your taste buds desire, as long as you keep within the budget.

There's No Right or Wrong Way to Plan Your Meals

Menu planning is not rocket science, so there's no right or wrong way to do it. What's important is that your family loves your recipes,

and that your food is healthy and within budget. While sticking to the plan is essential, it's crucial that your menu adapts to your family's changing taste buds. What use is a cheap menu if your family won't eat it?

With that in mind, start with the following tips on how to plan your meals a week ahead.

Take Stock Of What You Have

What do you do when you're buying a new dress? You probably look into your closet to see which colors and styles are already there so your new dress blends nicely into your existing wardrobe. Similarly, when planning for your menu, take stock of what you have in your fridge and cupboard. You may have the beginnings of pasta there, which you can then include in your menu for the week. Or, you may have ingredients that won't go well together by themselves, in which case you walk your fingers to your favorite food blog for inspiration. Other websites even allow you to put in whatever ingredients you have on hand, and then pull up recipes that make use of your existing ingredients with just a little addition from the garden or grocery.

Look For Bargains

It's unlikely that you have all the makings of a meal at first glance, so sooner or later you will have to hit the produce aisle to make a decent casserole. But before you do, it would save you serious money if you buy only what's in season or what's on sale.

Items on sale are usually "loss leaders," bargains that are barely making sales or breaking even to bait buyers into shopping at the store. At times, these are perishable goods nearing their "sell by" date that can be kept longer by storing them in the freezer.

Stocking up on these items is good strategy if you will be using said items anyway in the next few months. You will begin to see serious savings pile up if you plan your menu around these sales. You can always drive by the store to see if they have sale fliers available, or visit the store online to check their latest offerings. Once you've identified which ingredients or grocery items you will be needing in the next few weeks, comb through the fliers to match up your needs with the store's bargains. Then fill your cupboard and fridge to the brim.

Amidst all the sales buzz, you need, however, to exercise *buyer beware*. Simply because an item is on sale doesn't necessarily mean it's a great deal. Dig deeper and soon you will be more attuned to what really makes a great deal and how often such deals are offered in your area.

Match Up Sales With Your Coupons

Now that you have a clearer picture of what you have on hand and what you can grab for a discount, it's time to take out your coupons and put them to work. After listing down the items on sale that you wish to buy, match them up with your coupons and draw up your menu. You can find a list of little known places to find coupons on line here and here.

Menu Planning: Different Strokes for Different Folks

Menu planning is not set in stone. What might work for one family might not work with another. What your might family rave about this week might make them sick to the stomach the next. So keep trying new things every now and then while sticking to the budget. Find out what your family would like to eat that week, and see if you can cater to those wishes using ingredients that are on sale and in season.

In menu planning, no two weeks are going to be alike all the time. Some weeks you may have a lot of ingredients to work with, and lots of sales to comb through, while other weeks you might find that sales are scarce, your coupon clippings are few, and your fridge empty.

In times like that, you may want to consider freezer cooking. Freezer cooking is all about making all the ingredients in one huge batch, freezing them, and then cooking them when you are running out of ideas or new ingredients.

You can also use helpful spreadsheets that allow you to list down your grocery items with corresponding prices and coupons so you don't have to do it from scratch every time. There are plenty of websites you can download sales and coupons from. Make the most out of them, although you may need to find ones that, like your menu, will work best for you.

If you're really running low on coupons and sales are nowhere in sight, then you would have to work with what's left of your grocery money and use cookbooks or your favorite food blogs for inspiration.

Stick To Menus That Work For You

It's easy to waste 30 minutes in unproductive activities like getting lost down the Internet hole, so why not sit down and whip up a list of meals good for one month that your family would like to eat?

That would make a great start if you feel you're not up to making a menu at all.

If that doesn't work, you can always borrow ideas from others; the blogosphere overflows with such ideas. One example is to come up with themed dinners for each day of the week so that it's easier for you to streamline your menu when you're overwhelmed with options. You don't have to follow this to a T. The goal is to make room for anything that might pop up at the last minute, and keep ingredients for a quick meal within reach for when you are all running late and you just need a quick bite before you're desperate and hungry enough to dash for the nearest restaurant.

Meal planning doesn't always run smoothly though; expect to have some bumps along the way, especially if you are just new to it. Get motivated by the amount of savings you will enjoy over time (and how you can spend those savings), and you may just feel inspired enough to keep on track with menu planning, even if it was overwhelming when you started. To make the process a little more manageable, you can find some really good meal planning templates here and more detail about the actual "science" of meal planning here. Last, here's a great YouTube video with step-by-step instructions on creating a Google meal calendar.

Why You Need To Pay In Cash

When you're not paying your grocery with cash, it's easy to overshoot your budget, as it's easy to write off a $5 over budget expense when you swipe a debit or credit card. But paying $5 more every week on your grocery bill can easily add up to more than $100 a year. Paying with cash compels you to spend only whatever is in your envelope and nothing more. Of course, it's not going to always turn out that way, but at least you'll be less likely tempted to just charge it when you know you only have a certain amount to work with.

It's easy to overshoot your budget, especially when there are items that you think are a steal! But when you only have cash to pay, you tend to carefully evaluate the item, or you won't have any money left to pay for what's on your shopping list. You can take advantage of these sales, of course, but only when you can trade it off with something you can live without. If not, you can always put it back on the shelf.

The Challenge: Cash-Only Shopping

If you have long wondered why you always go beyond your grocery budget, now is the time to get creative and committed. To put you in this cash-only mindset, challenge yourself with the following:

- Stick to whatever cash you have in your grocery envelope for the next three months. It usually takes 8-10 weeks for new habits to become automatic, so after this time period you won't likely miss items you normally buy on impulse.
- Only withdraw cash that is equal to your grocery budget, which you then put in an envelope and stow away in a safe place.
- Bring only your cash when grocery shopping and nothing else. No debit/credit cards and no checkbook.
- Get a calculator and compute as you go. Doing so lets you see in black and white whether you still have room for something that's not on your grocery list but on your child's constant wish list. With a calculator, you'll know exactly how much you have left, and whether certain deals can still be accommodated. If your shopping list is longer, you can get creative by trading off certain items that have lower utility value.

- Pay only with cash. The goal is to eventually save, so pay only with cash and nothing else.
- Commit to not using your credit or debit card anymore to pay groceries. It may be hard to do this in the first few months, but sticking only to cash will teach you resourcefulness, because when you are constrained, you get creative.

Be a Savvy Money Manager Using Money Management Apps, Coupons, Promo Codes and Cash Back Sites

In budgeting as in life, knowing where you are at the moment and where you want to go is the definitive first step to becoming a savvier money manager. These days, with so many free tools online that increase our awareness of our spending habits, it's a huge waste if we don't put them to work to our financial advantage.

The Most Effective Money Management Apps

There are several ways you can cut back on your spending and start saving. Personal budgeting has always typically involved messy paperwork as you go through pockets and purses, so if removing paperwork will make it less painful for us to deal with money matters, then these touch-and-go apps should be downloaded on your mobile devices.

- **Mint.com.** You need iOS, Android and Windows on your device to get this free money management app. If you are more of a big-picture person, then this app is intuitively organized to let you take a glance and see where you are in your earnings, spending, saving and budgeting. Ideal for those who use debit or credit cards for their purchases, Mint alerts you when you are over-budget, shows you your cash flow in real time, and analyzes your spending patterns.

- **GoodBudget.** Previously known as EEBA, GoodBudget is a free app that works with iOS and Android devices. Even with this very modern touch, GoodBudget is charmingly old school as its envelopes system is similar to allocating cash into actual envelopes, building on the idea of divvying up your cash based on your cash flow. Ideal for those earning incomes on unpredictable schedules (such as freelancers), GoodBudget also lets you track your spending that is not recurring, like holiday gifts.
- **Mvelopes**. Mvelopes is more "personalized," as it asks you about your financial goals with a few simple questions, helping you think about money in the long-term. It has an envelope system similar to GoodBudget so you are forced to consider how much you have in your accounts versus what your budget could look like. Like Mint, this app directly tracks your debit and credit transactions by syncing up with your banks. It's free and works with iOS and Android.
- **Billguard.** Another free app for iOS and Android devices, Billguard is what it says on the label: it aims to protect your cards from fraudulent or unauthorized transactions. It also gives you a picture of your spending habits by syncing your bank accounts and bringing up your total balance and amount spent this month.
- **Pocket Expense.** A free app for iOS devices only, Pocket Expense gives you a snapshot of your spending patterns before creating budgets. Because it does not sync with your bank accounts, you have to manually enter amounts, first your checking and savings, then your spending. A highly visual app with color codes, Pocket Expense lets you track your expenses per day, week or month.
- **HomeBudget.** The "lite" version is free, but otherwise $4.99 on iOS and $5.99 on Android, HomeBudget features

easy-to-navigate categories: Expenses, Bills, Income, Budget, and Accounts presented in a color-coded chart. HomeBudget makes it easy for freelancers to track their incomes, and also makes it a breeze to search for a check received months ago from a specific client. A broader month-to-month look on your spending, budgeting and accounts is also available.

- **Expensify.** Another free app for iOS, Android and Windows, Expensify has easy-to-navigate features that work smoothly both on smartphone and web interfaces. There are four big buttons that let you do things: 1) SmartScan for when you want to photograph, categorize, tag receipts, and attach them to expense reports where necessary. 2) Add Expense lets you enter expenses manually and allows you to categorize them as either billable or reimbursable. 3) Track Time and 4) Track Distance are both useful for those who freelance, or travel by car and need to bill by distance. The web version of Expensify lets you input your debit and/or credit card, and shows you the small and big picture of your financial life.

Top Websites for Finding Coupons And Promo Codes

Latest surveys indicate that coupons remain a popular money-saving tool for consumers, and so businesses keep them in their marketing arsenal. And because they'll still be around, it's a wise budgeting move to browse the web for coupons and promo codes that will give you the best returns either in the form of discounts, free shipping, and buy-one-get-one (BOGO) deals. Here's a rundown of the top 10 websites where you can wade in an ocean of coupons and codes.

Brad's Deals

With over 4,000 retailers on its website, Brad's Deals makes an irresistible proposition. Sign up with its newsletter, and you'll get an alert about upcoming deals. If you have no time to view them now, the site will let you save your stores and deals for redemption later.

- **Coupons.com.** If you have a favorite store listed on Coupons, you just might get a loyalty coupon. If you are hunting for grocery discounts, this website makes an excellent resource.
- **Coupon Cabin. There** are 171,000 deals and coupons to be found on Coupon Cabin. If you shop from Target and The Home Depot, this site even offers cash back as well as from participating stores.
- **Hip 2 Save.** Hip 2 Save has it for people looking for a bit of variety. On top of freebies and coupons, you get exciting deals on restaurant offers, toys, and recipes, and news for rewards and sweepstakes.
- **The Krazy Koupon Lady.** Walmart, Amazon.com, Starbucks and Best Buy fans are going to go crazy with the tips, coupons and codes frequently updated on this website.
- **Passion for Savings.** If you are looking for printable coupons, Passion for Savings is a great place to find it. On top of freebies and deals, you also get to learn from this website general tips on how to save money.
- **Promocodes.com.** This site is what it says on the tin can. On top of offering coupons, the site focuses on aggregating promo codes, which you can then take advantage of using the "Trending Now" feature.
- **RetailMeNot.** Macy's, Eddie Bauer and Banana Republic are just some of the retailers in this site, which offers 500,000 coupons and codes. This massive database can be mined well using the search tool by category or by looking at special

pages made for each retailer. If you want to take advantage of international coupons, this is where you can find them.

- **Savings.com.** For shoppers who are more into tech and clothing as well as groceries, Savings has 200,000 deals to choose from. Look through the day's best deals to grab the best bargains, then put them on your "My Deals" tab. There is also a huge selection of printable coupons if you want to shop in-store.

- **Slick Deals.** When you want assurance from your fellow shoppers on the quality of coupons, Slick Deals is the place to go to. Editors put together a selection of deals, which the community rates and reviews. Site users also share their finds and any latest information about bargains.

The Best Cashback Sites For Online Shoppers

Cashback sites leverage the power of numbers. Operating on an affiliate basis with hundreds of online stores, cashback sites earn an affiliate commission when you buy from partner stores. The cashback sites then give a portion of that commission back to you as a reward.

You can't expect much from cashback rates, as it seldom goes above 10%. The benefit of using these sites though is that you can use them alongside sales, coupons and discounts, so in the end it all adds up to a decent discount off your purchases. Like websites for coupons and promos, cashback sites are plentiful, and here are some that have proven to be lucrative all these years.

- **Top Cashback.** If you are looking for a cashback site that's easy to use and navigate, gives you better rates than most sites, partners with a wide range of stores and pays cashbacks promptly, then Top Cashback is unbeatable. Plus you get a 2.5% bonus if you redeem your cashback for an Amazon credit code. It's not much, but if you're looking to cut your spending in ways that don't hurt, then small bonuses like this are always welcome. In addition, Top Cashback offers a $10 sign-up bonus paid out when you earn a corresponding amount in cashback.

- **Ebates.** When a merchant doesn't show up on Top Cashback, you might want to check with Ebates, one of the oldest cash-back sites since it opened in 1999, just a few years after the World Wide Web debuted. Generally, however, Ebates have slightly lower rates than Top Cashback's, but it's still a good idea to compare before you check out. The site's sign-up bonus is $10, which you get when you do a lot of shopping online within 90 days. You need to earn $25 in cashback in that time frame to claim the bonus.

- **Be Frugal.** For those particularly fond of shopping on Amazon. com, BeFrugal may just give them a better deal than the top two others. After a complete makeover of their site, BeFrugal is much easier to use, especially for hunting generous offer-ings like 30% cashback on Amazon magazines. Men's and women's shoes from Amazon may also win you another 8.5% cashback. As to the site's sign-up bonus, it works the same way as Ebates'.

Five Painless Ways To Save On Your Cell Phone Bill

We no longer "go online," we live online. As we do, cell phones have gone from nice-to-have to a necessity, and often an expen-sive one. It doesn't have to be, even as our devices have become deeply integrated into our daily lives.

As carriers compete with each other to keep old subscribers and attract new customers, there are bound to be some irresistible offers coming out every now and then in an attempt to win over customer loyalty from the other side of the fence. Take advantage of this, and you don't have to pay a three-figure monthly bill.

Yet a survey by financial services firm Cowen and Company shows that the average iPhone owner with one of the Big Four cellular providers (T-Mobile, AT&T, Sprint and Verizon Wireless) spends $111 a month, while others (excluding those using prepaid phones) pay $90 per month for individual service.

Cut The Multi-Year Contract

Users who are locked into two-year mobile phone contracts bear the brunt of paying exorbitant fees much higher than their actual consumption. With mobile phone trends rapidly changing, getting tied to a long-term commitment can really be costly. Two years is a long enough time to render even recently released devices obsolete.

Giant carriers are adapting to emerging trends, and are quickly pouncing on on-the-fence consumers by separating the cost of the device from the cost of monthly service. On the other end of the spectrum, smaller providers are finding novel and creative ways to push costs further down to the delight of those who defected to their camp.

Quality doesn't have to be sacrificed in the process of switching to a cheaper plan. Ting, Republic Wireless and Consumer Cellular are three upstart providers that are winning fans and earning top ratings in an annual survey on cell providers conducted by the Consumer Reports National Research Center from among their

63,352 subscribers. So far, Ting has earned the highest overall score.

There are plenty of ways to get your cell phone bill lowered to a reasonable rate. A good start would be to ditch your old phone and get a new one if you are planning to upgrade anyway. Other ways you can read below.

Get Out Of Your Existing Contract

With phones getting quickly outdated even after only a few years, it's not a wise financial move to get locked into the traditional two-year contract in exchange for getting the latest expensive smartphone for a small down payment. Consider paying for it over a period of two years on a zero-interest installment plan. It's cheaper, the line access fee is normally lower, and the down payment is often zero.

When you're locked into a multi-year commitment, you pay the same amount month after month even if your actual usage is much lower. With an installment plan, you get the latest device that you'll be able to use long after it's paid for, which is where the real savings begin. Even if your bill is only going to drop by $30 a month, that's still $360 a year in savings.

But how do you get out of a contract plan with a prohibitive early termination fee? You don't have to, at least not right away. Explore your current provider's cheaper alternatives and find out if you can downgrade with no extra charges. You should be able to investigate your options through your carrier's online portal.

If you wish to switch carriers instead, find out if the new provider will buy out your remaining contract period. They often do, in a bid to poach other carrier's customers. For example, T-Mobile and Sprint enticed new customers who wish to switch from another carrier and who brought their phones with them with a few hundred dollars per line. Sprint even cut in half the monthly rate for customers switching over from Verizon and AT&T.

Understand Your Data Needs

After dropping your old contract, it's time to find a better deal. Compute how much data each of your devices need, and then sign up for a data plan based on those needs. You can use a data measuring app like My Data Manager, your carrier's data calculator, and your old bills to help you figure out your average monthly usage. Take advantage of Wi-Fi connections, and you may not even need more than 2GB a month. If another device is not frequently using your cellular connection, you can free up between 4GB to 5GB a month that other devices in your network can use.

Compare Plans Of Giant Carriers

Big service providers have the advantage of huge infrastructure, reliable data network, and a large pool of knowledgeable customer service. If that's important to you, then compare plans offered by the Big Four. Verizon Wireless nails it across the board—text, voice, 4G reliability and Web. (In contrast, Sprint fares poorly in almost all measures.) AT&T leads the pack in 4G service. T-Mobile wins customer loyalty for its prompt issue resolution, staff knowledge, and the best prices among the big carriers. All have earned top marks for staff courtesy.

In short: T-Mobile for lower prices, Verizon for better across the board service and AT&T for excellent 4G data access (which suits most power smartphone users).

Go With Small Carriers

The most satisfied customers are usually those using the small providers who have the advantage of cheaper plans and more personalized service, which show in phone provider surveys.

Compare the three-digit monthly bill from the Big Four to the monthly bill you might pay with a smaller carrier. For three lines at only $80 a month, you already enjoy 2.5 GB of data, 15,000 text messages, and 1,200 voice minutes with Consumer Cellular. Thirty-five dollars ($35) more and you get a flip phone from the company. If you wish to get more recent models, you can do so for only $150 upfront and $25 a month for the next 20 months.

Small carriers tend to offer more flexible pricing, letting you pay only the actual data and minutes you use, which is the case with Ting. Ting has a pay-as-you-go plan that only requires a painless $6 access fee per line, unbelievably low rates of $9 for 500 minutes of voice, and $19 for 1GB of data. If you don't use up everything in the plan, you only pay for what you have actually used, and end up with a much lower bill.

Eliminate Data Hogs

● Be vigilant of your streaming habits and see where you can cut back; you may have signed up for a data package that's more than your actual need. To push your data usage further down, connect to a Wi-Fi network whenever you can. When you're on your cell network, minimize doing the following:

- Streaming music and video: Even a daily four-minute video stream from YouTube can easily add up to 700MB of data a month, the same amount of data if you were to stream your playlist during your half hour commute on weekdays and 20-minute workouts a few times a week. A high-definition video stream uses 5MB or 6MB a minute. Listening to your favorite songs consumes up to 1MB of data per minute.
- Making video calls: Video calling is heavy on your network.
- Uploading video: A three-minute HD-quality video clip (1080p) consumes up to 300MB of data. Unless extremely necessary, you can reduce the resolution so it's not going to be as heavy.
- Playing online games: fast action games with other online players consume 1MB of data per minute of play.

Now What? Five Cheaper Alternatives To Expensive Cell Phone Plans

The average monthly family and individual expenditures on cell phones range from $120 to $150 a month. Verizon Wireless customers, for example, paid an unbelievable $148 a month in the fourth quarter of 2013, according to research firm Cowen and Company. Other wireless giants such as Sprint, AT&T and T-Mobile charge their customers an average bill of $144, $141, and $120, respectively, for their cell and data service. While all these numbers include all taxes and fees, paying in the three digits is still expensive.

While some families may feel that the monthly cost of their cell and data plan is justified, (especially for those who may need to work from home occasionally or use multiple devices), the escalating cost of a monthly cell phone and data plan is getting to unreasonable levels, especially when you can get plans and quality of service comparable to large carriers at a fraction of the cost. Consider these providers:

Republic Wireless

No-contract plans are the way to go if you want to cut down your cell phone and data bill without significantly cutting back on the quality of service you enjoy. With Republic Wireless, it's possible to do this at only $5 to $40 a month; $25 already buys you unlimited Wi-Fi, talk, text, and data on 3G, one of their most popular plans.

The only thing you need is to have a Republic Wireless Android phone that lets you make calls on both Wi-Fi and cellular networks, which you can get for as low as $149 with their brand new Moto G phone. Everything is already included in your bill; what you sign up for is what you pay.

Ting

Paying only for the amount of service you use makes a lot of financial sense, and Ting allows you to do that for as cheap as $21 a month. This is because Ting has a pricing scheme that lets you "float" between plans while only billing you for your actual usage. So if your actual monthly use is 50 minutes and 100 texts, then you only pay for the price that that plan falls into. You can even add family members to your package for as low as $6 per device provided they are Sprint's.

Airvoice Wireless

You can further drive your bill down by bringing your own device compatible with Airvoice Wireless. For as low as $10 a month, you can already enjoy 500 text messages and 250 minutes of talk; $30 gets you unlimited plans with some data, but without a contract.

Straight Talk Wireless

You don't have to get locked into a long-term commitment that you are forced to pay even if your actual usage has dropped signifi-cantly. That's an alternative that Straight Talk Wireless provides. For only $30 a month, you may bring your own phone and even keep your old number as you switch to a new plan with unlimited data, talk and text.

Virgin Mobile Beyond Talk

Consumers on a budget may want to take advantage of Virgin Mobile's wide range of plans that include unlimited text and data with 300 minutes of talk for only $35 a month. There are no con-tracts to get tied up with, it's easy to keep your old number, and it's possible to get one of the low-cost phones without charge. You can even sign up with their Beyond Talk plan that starts in the $40 range if your phone is compatible with that plan.

The wide range of affordable yet quality phone and data packages make it costly to stick to a plan that bills upward of $100 a month. It is definitely worth an investment of your time and effort to explore low-cost options offered in your area, as it may take some time for prices to come down across the board—as it usually does when cell phone and data providers want to remain cut-throat competitive.

By cutting your bill down to a third of its usual amount, you'll see serious savings pile up before long, and you will be glad that you did your research.

4

Your Credit: What It Is, How To Fix It And How To Manage It

Your Credit: What It Is, How To Fix It, How To Manage It

For most people, credit is a complex subject, a dreaded task ranked next to filing taxes, which is a job best left to professionals. But don't be misled into believing that someone other than you is more qualified to fix your credit score at a speed faster than you can put down the hundreds, if not thousands, of dollars required to use a professional's services.

You don't need to be a credit consultant to repair your credit on your own. You don't have to go to school for it, nor be a financial expert. You just have to be willing to do the hard work that credit repair clinics claim they can do at lightning-quick speed. Because the truth is, only you can repair your credit yourself.

At best, credit repair clinics can legally do only those things that you yourself can do. At worst, they use questionable credit repair tactics—like stealing the Social Security number of a dead person—that can land you in more trouble than you initially started.

There are, of course, legitimate credit repair companies that can do the work for you. But remember, the only work they can do without violating any laws is the same work that you can do yourself, for which they will charge ridiculous amounts. That $5,000 you pay them for their unnecessary services is best used to pay down that old debt you thought had fallen off your credit report by now.

Considering the widespread financial ramifications of bad credit, you have no choice but to grit your teeth and bite the bullet. Patience, perseverance and postage are all you need to get your credit score from below the 500s to above the 720s. That, and an

ability to negotiate terms that are win-win for both you and the lender.

So don't ever fall for quick credit fixes. As with anything worth pursuing in life, fixing your bad credit yourself takes time. It may be a lot of work and a lot of overwhelming information you have to wade through, but persistence pays off. If you are lucky, you can see a significant jump in your credit score in as little as three months. Here's how.

Request for Your Free Credit Report

Despite the all-around importance of a credit score, some people don't bother checking theirs, even if it doesn't cost them nor negatively impact their numbers (getting your own report falls under "soft inquiries" that are not counted against your score).

Under the Fair and Accurate Credit Transactions Act, consumers are entitled to one free credit report each year from each of the three major credit bureaus – Equifax, Experian and TransUnion. You can pull your report from AnnualCreditReport.com, or you can call 1-877-322-8228.

Pulling your credit report from each credit bureau, even if all you intend to do is view it, is essential to make sure that your credit information is correct with the source so it will also be reported correctly to everyone who checks your credit references, which may not just be limited to companies you intend to get a loan from. Increasingly, some employers are opting to check their potential hires' credit report, even though the practice is not allowed in some states.

Audit the Items Carefully

Credit information comes from companies you have accounts with, so your goal, if you have credit repair in mind, is to make sure that inaccuracies are resolved and reflected in your credit score.

Auditing the entries is all the more important, as not all the three big national credit bureaus contain the same credit information. If you have a positive item reflected in your Experian report, make sure that is reflected in your other credit reports, too.

Also, remember that some debts can appear twice. How does this happen? It could be that your account with one company got delinquent, which was eventually sold off to a collections agency. So your original account (say, with Nordstrom for a pair of fancy shoes that you failed to pay off until it got delinquent) may appear as "purchased by another lender, unpaid balanced charged off," while the same account with the collections agency will appear as "placed for collection."

Both amounts will hit you twice, even though you only owe the debt to the collections agency after the original creditor sold it off. Unfortunately, these two amounts may not be listed side by side; the account with the original creditor may be listed on the first page, while the account sold off to the collections agency may be listed on the last, so it's going to be a challenging hunt for you to reconcile them.

But even if you don't need to fix your credit score, you still need to make sure that any inaccuracy is corrected. After all, if the erroneous entries pile up, they will eventually affect your score, and you will have to do the harder work of disputing each one of them.

Dispute Inaccurate Data

The U.S. Congress mandated a study on the credit report accuracy of the credit reporting industry. According to a Federal Trade Commission report, about 5% of consumers had errors on at least one of their three major credit reports. One in four consumers found errors on their credit reports that could affect their credit scores. One in five consumers, on at least one of their three credit reports, had errors that were corrected by a credit reporting agency after they were disputed.

An overwhelming four out of five consumers saw changes to their credit reports after they filed disputes. Of 250 consumers who filed disputes, one of them earned a maximum score change of more than 100 points (as opposed to 1 in 20 consumers getting a maximum score change of more than 25 points). If you are on the fence, those 100 points could tip the lending scales in your favor. It could mean the difference between getting a loan at a higher interest rate or the same loan at an easier rate.

Given these numbers, it's clear that consumers should pull their credit reports regularly, audit each item, and dispute accordingly. If consumers let errors go uncorrected, they pay for this oversight, literally: a low credit score not only translates to higher interest rates, but could even get your mortgage application denied, and with more and more employers looking into a candidates' credit records, your job application turned down.

Despite the myth, disputing inaccuracies on your credit report doesn't hurt credit score, nor do inaccuracies remain longer on your credit. Disputes are also not reported in your history, although any unresolved disputed item with your lender can be explained in a "Statement of Dispute" added to your credit report.

In a Statement of Dispute, you explain, in under 100 words, why the information is incorrect, as in "Never missed any payments with (name of the lender). The Statement of Dispute remains on your report for two years and can be seen by anyone who is allowed to review your report.

You can have one of the credit bureaus dispute an account on your behalf. Once a lender corrects a disputed item, it needs to report the correction to the reporting company it provided its data to.

Use a current copy of your credit report when disputing any item. You can use a variety of avenues to dispute incorrect information, from calling the phone number on your credit report, to using online apps from the credit bureaus. Keep in mind, however, that when disputing an item using the Internet, you may be giving up many of your rights. Giving up your rights can lead to exposing yourself possible identity theft, because reporting requires disclosure of confidential information (Social Security number, date of birth, etc.).

It's better to make your disputes via mail so you'll have a paper trail when it's time to gather your proof. To dispute inaccuracies, write a letter to each of the credit bureaus reporting the error. You can get a sample dispute letter from the Federal Trade Commission's website, where you can also learn about your rights (and perhaps those rights that you stand to give up when you dispute online).

Wait 30 Days for Response (or No Response) From Creditor

Once a creditor corrects a disputed item, the creditor must advise the reporting agency (i.e. Equifax, TransUnion, Experian) of the correction in order to update your credit profile. If the creditor fails to give a response within 30-45 days, the credit bureau will take out the entry or correct the negative information, and notify you of the results. If you do not agree with the results, you need to contact the creditor directly and provide additional documentation.

Verify Your Debts

When creditors claim that you owe them money, it's crucial to verify those claims, especially if they appear negatively on your credit report. Considering the massive amount of credit information creditors and credit bureaus have to deal with, it's not uncommon for mistakes—a simple clerical error is sometimes all it takes—to happen.

Verifying debts is important to establish whether the debt is really yours or not. This is not just inaccurate data; some entry on your credit report may not be altogether yours! While credit bureaus have an automated system called eOscar to help consumers sort disputes, what this system does is give you a code generated from a certain category code that may or may not have involved a live person calling a representative of the original creditor to check if the debt is really yours.

A more effective way to verify your debt is to send a Method of Verification letter to the credit bureau that reported an account "verified," which you feel is not based on your findings. It's simply an inquiry as to how an account was verified. The goal is to get a live person to pick up the phone and talk to someone about the account, not just generate a code after plugging a dispute into the eOscar system.

You may not get a response in the mail within the allotted 15 days, but you can check your report again and see if the unverified account has been removed.

Be Aware of Your State's Statute of Limitations

Additionally, verifying your debts is crucial, because of the statute of limitations on debt collection. The statute of limitations, which varies by state, declares that a debt collector can no longer pursue you for payment once a debt went unpaid for a certain period of time.

You may still have a moral obligation to satisfy old, unpaid debts, but the debt collector can no longer sue you over an unpaid debt that has lapsed beyond the statute of limitation in your state. Any collector who threatens to sue stands to violate the Fair Debt Collection Practices Act.

The statute of limitations (SOL) reckons from the date of first delinquency (DFOD). For example, you purchased an item in December, missed a payment in January, and paid again on time in February. Then you got delinquent again in March, and you haven't caught up since then. Your DFOD is that date in March. In the event you defaulted on that purchase altogether and it got sold to a collection agency, your SOL reckons from that DFOD and not from the date the account was sold to the collections agency.

Before you get comfortable with debts that have fallen off due to lapsed SOL, bear in mind the possibility of a judgment, which you should avoid by all means.

Getting positive items on your credit report is hard work, but getting judgment is rather easy. All you need to do is default and ignore collections. If the creditor really wants to get its money back, all it has to do is file papers with your local district court in small claims, and win the case (which they can handily do if you ignored the papers you were served). Even if this black mark were to fall off your credit report after seven years, you still will have a civil record for the next 10.

So while creditors can no longer report your debt after the SOL lapsed, they may still have time to file a judgment against you if your state's laws allow. In Illinois, for example, the SOL for written contracts is 10 years, but creditors there still have another 3 years to pursue the debt after it falls off your credit report. You may no longer have a legal obligation to settle your debts after the SOL lapsed, but you may still face the risk of getting a judgment that will follow you around for a really long time.

This is where your negotiating skills should come into full force. It doesn't matter if you settle the full amount or not; what matters is that the creditor agrees to it. If you can have the judgment "vacated," or removed from all records, all the better. The process involves appearing before a judge, telling your side of the story, and getting witnesses to vouch for you.

Validate Your Debts

Your debts have to be verified first before they can be validated. Verifying debts is altogether different from validating debts. It's a yes or no question: Do you owe a debt to a company? If no, you dispute it with the credit bureaus; if yes, then you have to validate with said creditor.

Validating your debt is getting proof—like credit slips signed by you—from the creditor that you indeed owe them an amount. This is crucial before any exchange of money is made.

Why is validating your debts extremely important? Because even if you know the debt is yours, the creditors may not have proof to be putting it on your report. Since this is a negative item on your report, which translates to a lower credit score, you want them to furnish proof before you start negotiations.

So if a debt is not verified, there is no debt to validate, which means that if you have checked with the original creditor first, you may be saved from the troublesome process of validating a debt that is no longer there to start with.

Send Your Debt Validation Letter

If your debt is verified, you want to validate it first before putting down any amount to satisfy your obligation. You can do this by sending out a debt validation letter either to the original creditor, or to the collection agency if your account with the original creditor was purchased.

There are plenty of debt validation letter samples you can find on the Internet, and you can get support and additional help from numerous forums that specialize in self-credit repair. (Just make sure that the information you put in is yours; you don't want to complicate matters by forgetting to take out information that is somebody else's.)

You should send out a debt validation letter every time you get a notice of a new collections account, and every time you acknowledge the debt is yours. Be sure to keep these letters so you will

have all your negotiations and requests in writing. Send your letters as certified mail with a return signature request. That way, you get a confirmation that the lender or collection agency received your debt validation request.

Hold on to this certified mail receipt/signature card, because it's crucial. Why? Once you get the confirmation that the creditor received your letter, it has 30 days from the date it received your letter to reply to your request for validation. If it fails to respond, it is in violation of the Fair Credit Reporting Act, and it no longer has a right to put the negative item on your credit report.

So once you sent out your mail, it's all a waiting game. Give it a few days for the mail to get to the creditor. Once you receive the validation and proof of debt, you can start to negotiate. Maybe you can settle for a deletion, wherein you pay the total amount owed in exchange for the creditor to remove the negative item from your report. If you can get it to do that, get those terms in writing in the mail before you pay anything.

Start paying off smaller debts, or ones that are nearing their statute of limitations. If you are fortunate, the creditor or collection agency won't reply, and you can then send a letter to the credit bureaus requesting the removal of "invalidated" debts.

Make Good Use of "Goodwill Adjustments"

If the negative entries on your credit report, such as late payments on a credit card, are accurate and validated, then you have to work at removing these items to improve your credit score.

Regardless of the reason why you missed a payment (maybe you had a real financial difficulty at that time, or were recovering from an illness), delinquencies can have widespread financial impact, not only in terms of late fees and higher annual percentage rates (APRs), but more important, your ability to qualify for future loans with low interest rates.

This is where you can bank on a creditor's goodwill through a goodwill letter. The creditor is not obliged to extend this to you, but if you are lucky, you can get an agent from a creditor or collection agency who empathizes with your situation and removes the black mark on your report.

A convincing goodwill letter is courteous (even if you are writing to correct their clerical mistake), has an appreciative tone, contains relevant documents to support your claim, is simple, and takes responsibility for any delinquencies. As well, there are plenty of samples of these online that you can customize according to your unique circumstances.

If you still have an account with this creditor, it helps to have a decent payment history to gain its trust and to show it that the delinquency that happened is not a pattern. (Otherwise, it's difficult to convince the creditor that you are taking responsibility for the late payment.)

Use the address you find on your credit report or on the creditor's website to send your goodwill letter to. While it is not legally bound to respond to your request, following up with the bureau multiple times via multiple communication channels may wear it down and make it relent.

Request Removal of Invalidated Debts

Failure of the creditor or collection agency to furnish proof that you owe it something no longer gives it the right to report that debt to your credit report. You want to let the credit bureaus know that you have written a debt validation letter, which the collection agency failed to respond to. You will send a letter of request to remove said item from your report to each of the credit bureaus— Experian, TransUnion and Equifax. (Remember, each one of them generates your credit report independent of the others.)

There are plenty of credit bureau sample letters online that you can fashion one after and customize it with your unique circumstances. Always ensure that the information you plug into the sample letter is yours to avoid complications.

Like the debt validation letter, you have to send these requests via certified mail with a return signature request. Keep those signature cards once more, because again, it's a waiting game from the moment you receive those cards.

Like the collection agencies, the credit bureaus have 30 days to respond to your request. Some of them may send you back a letter; some may not. This is where credit-monitoring websites come into use. You may pull your report monthly to check if your report has reflected your request. "Soft" inquiries do not affect your credit score, so it's worth requesting a fresh report to keep track of changes.

It can be challenging to figure out at first how to go about repairing your credit yourself. The process definitely demands a lot of communication, patience to wait and negotiation skills. Given how these three little numbers rule your life, it's definitely a battle worth fighting.

Managing Your Credit: Why it's Important and What You Can do to Improve Your Score

It may be a simple three-digit number, but your credit score can determine a lot of things in your life. Whether you are aware of it or not, your credit score either makes it hard or easy for you to get loans—housing, cars and even insurance – and if so, at what rates.

In fact, your credit report might even be used to determine your "hire-ability," no matter how controversial this practice is, and even prohibited in 11 states. While employers cannot request your credit report without your permission, this hiring practice is more prevalent than one might suspect. In a 2012 survey by the Society for Human Resource Management, almost 50% of employers check applicants' credit reports (credit scores can't be released for employment screening purposes) as part of the hiring process.

If you look at it closely, your credit history reflects how trustworthy and responsible you are as a person. It's to an employer's advantage, therefore, to only hire people who can be depended on to perform the duties he or she agreed to.

Especially if the hiring is done for a sensitive position (such as a cashier or finance officer or a purchasing manager), it stands to reason that a company would only want to bring people on board who can be trusted professionally and personally. Theft and embezzlement are real threats to a company's financial security, so it's no wonder that companies would want to make sure their employees can be entrusted with company resources.

Because of its inescapable importance in our lives, it's only prudent to manage our credit diligently; being negligent with it can lead to bankruptcy (and to all the negative things associated with bankruptcy, even after you've come out of it clean). To make sure you don't fall into that trap, here are some of the tips to help keep your head above the water.

Stay on Top of Your Credit Score

Considering how this three-digit score could impact your life, it's only proper to give it due importance by monitoring it regularly. Request your credit report from the Big Three national credit bureaus—Experian, Equifax and TransUnion—to make sure there are no errors. Requesting your own report falls under the "soft inquiry" category and won't affect your numbers.

Understanding Your FICO Score

Making the Grade: What Your FICO Score is Made of and Why it Matters

Your creditworthiness, or the likelihood that you will pay back your credit obligations as agreed, is measured by your credit score. That, in turn, is largely based on your FICO score.

Your FICO score is calculated by a predictive analytics company called Fair Isaacs Corporation (hence, the shorthand FICO) using data on your credit reports at the three major credit bureaus. FICO, the corporation, is not a credit-reporting agency like Experian, Equifax and TransUnion, but a company that develops algorithms used to generate your scores, and provides those algorithms to the credit bureaus.

FICO Score: Industry Standard for Over 25 Years

Your credit score may also use some other scoring algorithms like VantageScore, which other (smaller) credit reporting bureaus might use for the same purpose as your FICO score is used. But the FICO score has been widely used by almost 90% of lenders in the United States, and it remains the score that lenders refer to when approving a mortgage on your house, a car loan, or another credit card.

Because the Big Three have been using the FICO score to summarize your credit risk, the credit score you have come to know (or hate) is essentially a FICO score.

Whether you are actively monitoring your credit score or not, this three digit-number has played an all-encompassing role in your life, so it's worth a little effort to take the time to understand how it's calculated, and how it can make a huge difference not just in your finances, but even in your personal life.

580 and Below Need Not Apply

FICO, the company, develops an algorithm that computes your creditworthiness based on data available to the credit bureaus, which they use to assign borrowers a score between 300 and 850. For you to get approved on most loans, you need to have a score in the upper 700s. A score of 760 or higher puts you in the top-tier of any loan you might wish to apply for. The national average is 695.

The highest FICO score one can get is 850. And yes, as elusive as that number may appear, one very obsessive consumer earned the perfect score, not just with one credit bureau, but with all the

Big Three. If it was done once, it certainly can be done again. That is certainly a feat worth duplicating, but should you go to the trouble? Use the following table and you decide.

FICO Score	Rating	What It Means to Lenders
800+	Exceptional	Exceptional borrower who is likely to pay all her debts according to the agreed-upon terms
740-799	Very good	Dependable borrower likely to pay her debts.
670-739	Good	A good score within or a little above the Average US con-Sumer (a score that will likely get you one foot in the door.
580-669	Fair	Quite risky but still eligible for some loans.
Below 580	Poor	A really risky borrower

Interestingly, even with these black-and-white numbers to help lenders decide who is a good credit risk and who is not, a good FICO score varies by lender and by industry. One lender may offer the lowest interest rate to an applicant with a score of 730 or better, while another may make the cut-off at 760.

Industry-specific FICO scores have a score range of 250-900, using a FICO score version tailored to their needs. For example, auto lenders require a FICO score of 726, housing lenders look for 738, and credit card lenders make the cut-off at 723.

You Have More Than One Score

Don't be surprised if your FICO score is not the same across the board; meaning, your Experian score may be different from that of your TransUnion, which can be different from your Equifax credit score. This is because each bureau generates and updates your credit report based on public record and lender-provided information.

Similarly, your lenders may or may not look at all three of your scores, although mortgage lenders tend to take into account all three, while credit card issuers generally look at just one. This means that the bigger the loan that is at stake, the more intense the scrutiny your creditworthiness is going to take.

How Lenders Use Your Score

FICO scores make the lending process faster and fairer for con-sumers: by using a three-digit number that everyone is sub-jected to, lenders can compare apples with apples, and oranges with oranges. Without FICO scores, how should lenders decide which loan gets approved, and at what rates? Maybe they can use some other means to objectively determine a person's credit risk, but without a standard in place, loan processing is going to be time-consuming, because credit investigation will be painstaking.

A low FICO score does not automatically disqualify you from a loan (because then banks will have a much smaller market). You may still avail of a loan, but at rates higher than those with scores bet-ter than you. A FICO score, therefore, is a lender's convenient tool to segment the market to help borrowers get access to the credit they deserve.

So How Does The FICO Formula Work?

Considering the sensitivity of information involved in the computation of your credit score, the actual formula for determining your creditworthiness is a tightly guarded secret. But the broad strokes have been made available, so if you want to gain insight on how to increase your score, or how to repair your credit on your own, you will have to understand how the five categories of information that make up your FICO score are given relative weight.

Payment History

Since FICO uses predictive analysis to determine the likelihood of your ability to pay a debt, it's not surprising that your payment history makes up 35% of your FICO score. Payment history is all about whether you are paying your bills on time each month. So if you keep track of your monthly dues and pay them "before" rather than "on" the due date, then 35% of your score will take care of itself.

This is why consumers who only use cash for most of their transactions run the risk of lowering their credit scores. Because cash payment is not recorded in your credit history, the credit bureaus have no data to work on to arrive at scoring this category.

Length of Credit History

To make forecasts, analysts look at past behaviour in an attempt to predict future behaviour. So if you've been a diligent payer in the last 10 years, the likelihood that you will pay your bills on time for the foreseeable future is high.

To come up with your score for length of credit history, which makes up 15% of your FICO score, analysts look at the age of your oldest account, the average age of your credit accounts, and the ages of each accounts.

This category explains why your score might drop by a significant point if you pay off and cancel a credit card you had from way back. For example, if your oldest account was from 10 years ago, and your second oldest account is from 5 years ago, if you close the decade-long credit account, you may only be left with more recent credit that can earn you negative points three ways: shorter length of credit history, increased ratio of new credit versus old credit, and reduced loan availability.

Amounts Owed

When you close an old credit account, you effectively reduce the amount of loan that is made available to you. For example, if your combined credit limit from all your credit cards is $20,000, and you closed an old credit card that has a limit of $5,000, your available credit limit will only be $15,000.

Assuming that on that $15,000, you still owe $10,000, then the amount you owe relative to your available credit is 66.67%. Had you kept the old credit card, that figure would have been only 50% ($10K divided by $20K). Because your FICO score decreases as your amount owed relative to available credit increases, you wouldn't want to close accounts that have high credit limits.

Inversely, you need to keep your outstanding balance low by paying your debts regularly. For comparison, a customer who has an outstanding debt of $500,000 on a mortgage which was originally for $1 million (50% paid off) would earn higher marks in this category than someone who owes $100,000 on a $120,000 mortgage (16.67% paid off). Ideally, you want to use up only up to 20% of your credit limit to look good in this category.

Mix of Credit Accounts

If all your life you only had credit cards and nothing else, you're potentially decreasing your FICO score by (no more than) 10%. While you may have spotless credit history when it comes to credit cards (which are unsecured), you may not have the same credit-worthiness when it came to mortgage or auto loan. This is why your FICO score takes into account the variety of credit you've managed over the years.

The reasoning behind this is that the more varied your debts and the more adept you were at managing them (as reflected in your account's good standing), the likelier you are going to be able to manage other debt obligations such as secured loans. Secured loans are loans guaranteed by your house or car, which the lender can repossess in case of default.

This is also the reason why your credit score takes a hit when you cancel your credit card and you are left with only auto loans and mortgage. You will have a lower mix of credit accounts that analysts can use to forecast your future credit performance.

New Credit

It's not uncommon for people in deep debt to borrow from one account to pay another. That behavior is likely to show in the new credit category when you try to open one credit account to keep current with another. This means that the more you've applied for credit within the past year, the lower your score will be in this category, which makes up 10% of your FICO score.

How do the credit bureaus know that you are attempting to get more credit? Every time a lender pulls up your credit score, that takes a hit because lender inquiries are hard inquiries (as opposed to 'soft' inquiries that you make when you pull up your report) that lower your score.

If you're successful opening up a new credit account, that too goes in the computation. When your new accounts "age," and your inquiries get further into the past, your credit score is going to improve as this category gets a higher score.

A Word About Credit Repair Clinics

Knowing which ingredients and how they are mixed get into the credit score pot, you're in a better position to improve your score even if you do it on your own. Credit repair clinics abound and promise to get you from 500s to 700s, and they may be able to do it.

But here's the caveat: credit repair clinics, even the most reputable ones, can only legally do so much for you that you could have done for yourself. Steer clear of individuals or businesses who claim to be experts and promise to fix bad credit and make it good. In all likelihood, they are using underhanded—if not outright illegal— methods to get your credit score to where you hope it could be.

Is it Possible to Achieve a Perfect Score?

Interestingly enough, no two credit scores are ever alike, even if they're your own. As previously mentioned, your credit scores from the Big Three are not at all the same, because they assign your creditworthiness grade based on the information they have available on you.

If that is not complicated enough, the FICO scores themselves have several versions, the latest of which is FICO 9, which attempts to take into account medical debts (a headache in themselves) and paid collections (more headache). Much like software, the earlier versions appear to be more favored by lenders. The majority of them still use FICO 8 or earlier.

In the world of US financial services, 850 is the magic number, a score that is a steep climb, but not impossible to achieve. And while you want to have stellar credit that will put you first in line in the pecking order of loan approval and open doors to perks that are non-existent for low scorers, it's not necessary, nor practical, to strive for the perfect score.

True, you will impress anyone who checks your credit, but having 850 will not get you a better rate than someone with an 800. Nor will your 850 open more credit opportunities than someone with a score 30 points lower. You should only start to worry when you are bordering on 760, because that is the minimum score that will get you the top-tier treatment for almost all loans available to borrowers.

Exercise Caution with a Cushion

Still, you want to leave a comfortable cushion in case some agent forgot to remove the collection item from your credit report after you have settled for the "pay for delete" deal. After all, you can easily fall from your high chair by as much as 50 points by maxing out one of your credit cards, or 25 points by paying off your only credit card and leaving it with no revolving balance.

Horror stories do happen in the financial services industry, and sometimes these errors find a way to get into your credit report. So while 850 should be more of an aspirational score than a score that you should actually go after, it definitely pays to have a generous margin in case unforeseen actions penalize you with a significant drop in points.

How to Boost Your FICO Score

A perfect FICO score is definitely nice to have if only it were not that difficult to achieve. But you can maximize your score so you will have enough cushion in case life throws something at you and you weren't able to bounce back. How?

Consciously make decisions that will boost your score. Use what you learned about categories and their weights the next time you are on the hunt for new credit, or itching to cut up your credit card because of its soaring interest rates. (Transfer balances to a card with teaser rates instead.)

You may also want to emulate the behavior of those who earned high marks and customize what you learned to your unique circumstances.

In the case of one consumer who simultaneously earned 850 FICO scores from the Big Three, he had one active revolving credit card account, one active installment loan like a mortgage, no credit inquiries within the past year, and no new revolving credit card account in 10 years. He also knew exactly the due dates on his credit card statements and the dates when they reported balances.

A perfect FICO score requires a "perfect storm" of credit strategy and life situations, which everyone may not be privileged to have in one lifetime. Still, it doesn't mean you cannot join the FICO High Achievers club, a group of people who share common characteristics when it came to, say, their payment history. These characteristics are:

- No missed payments (about 96% of them)
- No collections listed on their report (only 1% have)
- No public record listed on their credit report

That said, how do you get listed on the public record? These following actions appear on the public record and collection items:

- Bankruptcies
- Foreclosures
- Suits
- Wage attachments
- Liens and judgments

While it's a challenge to get a 720, let alone a perfect score, it's not that difficult to get listed on the public record by way of getting a judgment. All you have to do is default on a payment, let it go to collections, ignore collections, and get a summons.

You don't want to be listed on the public record. By all means, pay off items that have gone to collection, or fell off your report after the statute of limitations, even if you no longer have a legal obligation to settle them.

As you can see, those items can bite you back and leave a nasty mark, so hunker down and pay down your debts while you are ahead. Your credit score is an all-important number that will follow you for the rest of your life, so it's worth going to a lot of trouble to make it exceptional.

How to Increase Your FICO Score

Keep Your Balances Low

Do you know that 30% of your credit score is calculated based on your outstanding debt? This means that the higher your outstanding debts, the lower your credit score will be. This often happens when you have several cards approaching their limit, thus lowering your available credit. To increase your credit score, bring down your card balances to 25% or less of their limits.

Request a Higher Limit

Alternatively, if you are close to maxing out, it might help to request for a higher limit. The goal is to expand your available credit and consequently improve your credit score. But tread gently when going this route: making a request like this could trigger the lender into pulling your credit report, which then becomes a "hard" inquiry that negatively affects your credit score.

But don't be tempted to use up this available credit to tack on more credit, which won't do your score any good at all. You have to be very disciplined not to use this available credit as an excuse to spend beyond what you can afford.

Take Advantage of Lower Rates

While you're on the phone with an agent, inquire if you can qualify for a lower interest rate, especially if you've been prompt with your payments.

As always, you have to read the fine print before transferring balances, especially if you are doing it with another credit card issuer. You might incur surcharges for transferring balances, and the interest rate after the introductory period may not turn out to be favorable after all. Worse, getting a lower interest rate is not worth taking a hit to your credit score, unless you have a solid number—about 700 or higher—to begin with.

Take on New Debts Only When Necessary

Transferring one card's balance to another is essentially taking on new debt, and opening new credit lines negatively impact your score because of "hard inquiries" that potential lenders are going to make to check your credit score. While new credit only makes up 10% of your score, that percentage could mean the difference if you are bordering on 700.

Close Your Accounts Only When There's Good Reason

Closing accounts equates to reducing your available credit and will potentially hurt your credit score in the short term. There's actually no need to close accounts that have good payment history and a low outstanding balance. Remember, 35% of your credit score comes from your payment history. If you close these accounts, you are deleting some of this good history.

In addition, 10% of the score comes from available credit, so the smaller available credit you have, the lower your credit score could potentially be.

Plus, if this credit has been around for a long time, not only will you be erasing good credit history, but also the length of that history. You get 15% of your score from the length of time you've had credit, which means that the longer you've had established credit, the more information is available about your past payment history , and the more accurate is the prediction of your future actions.

Be Vigilant About Your Debt-to-Income (DTI) Ratio

Debt-to-income ratio is not directly related to the computation of your credit score, but it does have implications when it comes to your ability to pay. The higher your DTI, the lower your potential to pay past and future loans. If you are over your head with credit right now, budget mercilessly and find a way to open up another stream of income that will make you more liquid.

Pay Before Your Due Date

Don't pay "on" a bill's due day; rather, pay *before*. Don't wait until the last hour to send in your payments, as unforeseen events may get in the way of you sending in your payments on time. Remember, your payment history makes up 1/3 of your credit score, and any tardiness will be reflected in that history. On top of that hit, you will also be paying late fees and other surcharges, which is well within your power to avoid.

Pay Off in Full Each Month

Revolving your credit is expensive in terms of charges you need to pay and of the hit that your credit score is going to take. So clear your balance whenever you can. It increases your available credit, it saves you interest and late fee charges, and in case of emergency, that available credit will come in handy in case you incur expenses that are higher than anticipated.

Set Up a Direct Debit

If something is convenient to do, you are likely to do it more. By having money go out of your bank account automatically, you won't feel the pain of money getting in your hands only to be leaving soon. What you don't see, you won't miss.

Get Out of Recurring Payments on Your Credit Card

Recurring payments are also known as continuous payment authority, which means that a company can put charges on your credit card automatically. For example, if you are subscribed to a music streaming service that automatically bills you every month, it's a better idea to have that automatic billing come out of your debit card than your credit card.

The reason? If you are not aware of your available credit, you might accidentally go over your limit even without your consent (because with a CPA [Continuous Payment Authority, referred to in previous sentences], you've already given prior consent), leading to charges that you could have avoided in the first place. Call your card provider and let it know that you are withdrawing your CPA.

Review Your Purchases

Checking your monthly card bill serves two purposes: to monitor your spending habits, and to ensure that all purchases are reflected in your bill correctly. Call your card issuer's customer service for any erroneous billing.

Avoid the Minimum Payment Syndrome (MPS)

The minimum payment figure was designed to be small enough to be painless to card holders so they continue paying that amount over the long term, which is where the banks make the most money. And because paying the minimum is convenient, many consumers fall into the MPS (minimum payment syndrome) trap.

By the time they've paid off their loan on a minimum payment amount, it would have likely tripled, courtesy of compound interest. Bite the bullet instead and fork in more than the minimum amount so you pay down your debts quickly on an interest rate that doesn't border on usurious.

Sign Up for Reward Cards

One way to fund some of your expenses is to convert your credit card points into rewards, say for miles or cash back. Especially if you are a diligent payer, there's no reason why you can't get an airline frequent flier card and enjoy the perks. For frequent shoppers, a cash back rewards card might be more appropriate.

If you pay your balance in full every month, use your credit card as a method of payment. Charge your purchases on your credit card, and use cash to pay your card to rack up points.

Protect Your Transactions

Even with increasingly sophisticated encryption, identity theft is still a common occurrence, especially among those who are not careful with their personal information.

While not directly affecting your credit score, having your identity stolen could mean that your personal information can be used to obtain credit. Fixing the damage caused by identity thieves can be a very time-consuming and expensive process, not to mention psychologically aggravating. Avoid identity theft by all means— preventing it is a lot less painless than undoing the damage.

Protect Yourself from Identity Theft

What is Identify Theft?

Identity theft occurs when someone uses another person's personal information such as name, Social Security number, driver's license number, credit card number or other identifying information to take on that person's identity in order to commit fraud or other crimes.

How to Protect Yourself from Identity Theft

The following tips can help lower your risk of becoming a victim of identity theft.

- Protect your Social Security number. Don't carry your Social Security card or other cards that show your SSN. Read, "Your Social Security Number: Controlling the Key to Identity Theft" (http://www.socialsecurity.gov/pubs/10064.html).
- Use caution when giving out your personal information. Scam artists "phish" for victims by pretending to be banks, stores or government agencies. They do this over the phone, in e-mails and in postal mail.
- Treat your trash carefully. Shred or destroy papers containing your personal information including credit card offers and "convenience checks" that you don't use.
- Secure your wallet or purse at all times.
- Do not share passwords with friends or family.
- Protect your postal mail. Retrieve mail promptly. Discontinue delivery while out of town.
- Check your bills and bank statements. Open your credit card bills and bank statements right away. Check carefully for any unauthorized charges or withdrawals and report them immediately. Call if bills don't arrive on time. It may mean that someone has changed contact information to hide fraudulent charges.
- Check your credit reports. Review your credit report at least once a year. Check for changed addresses and fraudulent charges.
- Stop pre-approved credit offers. Pre-approved credit card offers are a target for identity thieves who steal your mail. Have your name removed from credit bureau marketing lists. Call toll-free 888-5OPTOUT (888-567-8688).
- Ask questions. Ask questions whenever you are asked for personal information that seems inappropriate for the transaction. Ask how the information will be used and if it will be shared. Ask how it will be protected. If you're not satisfied with the answers, don't give your personal information.
- Protect your computer. Protect personal information on your computer by following good security practices.

- Use strong, non-easily guessed passwords.Use firewall, anti-virus, and anti-spyware software that you update regularly.
- Download software only from sites you know and trust, and only after reading all the terms and conditions.
- Don't click on links in pop-up windows or in spam e-mail.
- Use caution on the Internet. When shopping online, check out a website before entering your credit card number or other personal information. Read the privacy policy and take opportunities to opt out of information sharing. Only enter personal information on secure web pages that encrypt your data in transit. You can often tell if a page is secure if "https" in the URL, or if there is a padlock icon on the browser window. This is a small but important point; before you buy something online and give out personal data and credit card numbers, look for https and a green padlock icon in your browser. That's green for go, and https, not http.

When Your Data Has Been Compromised or Stolen

When you become aware of an identity breach, it's important to immediately close any accounts that were opened in your name as soon as possible. Also, check on your legitimate accounts to make sure that details like mailing addresses have not been changed by someone else.

Credit Reporting Agencies

If you have reason to believe your personal information has been compromised or stolen, contact the fraud department of one of the three major credit bureaus listed below.

Equifax
Direct Line for reporting suspected fraud:
800-525-6285
Fraud Division
P.O. Box 740250
Atlanta, GA 30374
800-685-1111 / 888-766-0008
http://www.equifax.com

Experian
Direct Line for reporting suspected fraud:
888-397-3742
Credit Fraud Center, P.O. Box 1017
Allen, TX 75013
888-EXPERIAN (888-397-3742)
http://www.experian.com

TransUnion
Direct Line for reporting suspected fraud:
800-680-7289
Fraud Victim Assistance Department
P.O. Box 6790
Fullerton, CA 92634
Phone: 800-916-8800 / 800-680-7289
http://www.transunion.com

When contacting the Credit Reporting Agency, you should request the following:

- Instruct them to flag your file with a fraud alert including a statement that creditors should get your permission before opening any new accounts in your name.
- Ask them for copies of your credit report(s). (Credit bureaus must give you a free copy of your report if it is inaccurate because of suspected fraud.) Review your reports carefully

to make sure no additional fraudulent accounts have been opened in your name, or unauthorized changes made to your existing accounts.

NOTE: In order to ensure that you are issued free credit reports, we strongly encourage you to contact the agencies' DIRECT LINES (listed above) for reporting fraud. We do not recommend that you order your credit report online.

- Be diligent in following up on your accounts. In the months following an incident, order new copies of your reports to verify your corrections and changes, and to make sure no new fraudulent activity has occurred.
- If you find that any accounts have been tampered with, or opened fraudulently, close them immediately. To ensure that you do not become responsible for any debts or charges, use the ID Theft Affidavit Form developed by the Federal Trade Commission to help make your case with creditors.

Social Security Administration
SSA Fraud Hotline: 800-269-0271
http://www.ssa.gov/

If you are the victim of a stolen Social Security number, the SSA can provide information on how to report the fraudulent use of your number and how to correct your earnings record. We encourage you to contact the SSA Fraud Hotline immediately once you suspect identity theft.

The website also provides tips on using and securing your Social Security number. Visit the SSA website for advice on keeping your number safe.

ID Theft Clearinghouse
1-877-ID-THEFT (1-877-438-4338)

Call the ID Theft Clearinghouse toll-free to report identity theft. Counselors will take your complaint and advise you how to deal with the credit-related problems that could result from identity theft.

Local Law Enforcement

It is important that you report identity theft to your local police department as soon as you become aware that you are a victim. Get a copy of the police report, which will assist you when notifying creditors, credit reporting agencies and if necessary, the Social Security Administration (SSA).

Resources

The following links provide detailed information related to identity theft and protecting yourself.

Identity Theft Resource Center
http://www.idtheftcenter.org/

Department of Justice
http://www.justice.gov/criminal/fraud/websites/idtheft.html

Federal Trade Commission
http://www.consumer.gov/idtheft/

Social Security Administration
http://www.socialsecurity.gov/pubs/10064.html

Privacy Rights Clearinghouse - Identity Theft Resources
http://www.privacyrights.org/identity.htm

Pennsylvania Commission on Crime and Delinquency - Identity Theft Action Plan
http://www.identitytheftactionplan.com

What to Do if Someone Has Already Filed Taxes Using Your Social Security Number
http://turbotax.intuit.com/tax-tools/tax-tips/General-Tax-Tips/Identity-Theft--What-to-Do-if-Someone-Has-Already-Filed-Taxes-Using-Your-Social-Security-Number/INF23035.html

List of Identification Theft Protection Service Providers
http://www.reviews.com/identity-theft-protection-services/

National Fraud Information Center Hotline: 800-876-7060
Identity Theft Resource Center: 858-693-7935

Debt Avalanche vs. Debt Snowball: Which Is The Best Way To Pay Off Debt?

Now that you've begun the work to repair your credit, the next step is managing your current debt. There are two universally accepted methods of paying down debt: the Debt Snowball Method and the Debt Avalanche. Which one is better, the Debt Snowball or the Debt Avalanche? I'm from the school of thought that the best method is a combination of the two. So, just how can you combine these methods to get out of debt? Read on to find out.

Let's make sure we understand exactly how these two methods differ. The Debt Snowball and the Debt Avalanche are the two main strategies for paying down your debt. The Debt Snowball method says you should start by paying off the credit cards or loans with the lowest balances first, while the Debt Avalanche method tells you to pay off the accounts with the highest interest rates first.

First, a metaphor.

Imagine you're a firefighter and are called to save a burning house. You enter the house, and see two main areas of fire: two burning logs in one corner, and five burning fuel tanks in another. The logs are bad, but the fuel tanks are wreaking havoc. Which do you put out first?

Most people's gut reaction is obvious: put out the tanks. Those things are going to blow up.

However, if these two groups of burning objects were your debts, the snowball method would tell you to put out the logs first, because there are fewer of them (only two!) Then, after an early victory, you move on to the fuel tanks.

The avalanche method would tell you to put out the fuel tanks first, because they are more flammable and spreading fire faster. Here's the reality: *Your high interest debts are like those fuel tanks, burning down your financial house.* Due to compound interest, they cause much more damage than low interest debt, no matter what size the debts are.

The Current Debate

Most people will tell you that your strategy is a choice, depending on what you value most while paying off debt: (1) overall speed and savings, or (2) sustained motivation. (But you can't have both).

Dave Ramsey has made the Debt Snowball famous and has championed it for years. He says it's the best way because it helps you build up momentum by paying off the accounts with lowest balances first. You get quick wins by paying off accounts, and this

makes you more likely to stick with your plan. After all, saving money is great, but it's not gonna happen if you can't stick with a plan long-term. However, proponents of the Debt Avalanche point out that you can lose *thousands* of dollars by choosing not to tackle your highest interest accounts first.

How Big Is The Difference, Really?

Say you have the following debts:

Student Loan: $15,000 balance, 4.5% interest rate
Auto Loan 1: $5,000 balance, 12.99% interest rate
Personal Loan 2: $25,000 balance, 29.99% interest rate

If we assume you can pay $3,000 per month to get out of debt, your debt payoff timeline using the Snowball method would look like this:
Debt Snowball. Total interest paid: **$9,416.16**

So you would be entirely debt free by May 2013, and you would pay a total of $9,416 in interest. Ouch.

Now let's look at what your timeline would be with the Avalanche:
Debt Avalanche: Total interest paid: **$5,979.26**

Using the avalanche, you would be debt free by March 2013, a whole two months earlier, and you would save $3,436 in interest!

Let's say that again: just paying your debts in the wrong order in this situation would have cost you over three thousand dollars. (You can run the numbers on your own finances here.

The difference may be larger or smaller, but the Debt Avalanche always wins in terms of time and money saved. Clearly, it's the more financially logical way to pay off your debts.

So assuming you stick with your plan, the Avalanche method is superior. However, we can't forget about the emotional aspect of paying down your debts. According to Dave Ramsey when recommending the Snowball, "the math seems to lean more toward paying the highest interest debts first, but what I have learned is that personal finance is 20% head knowledge and 80% behavior. You need some quick wins in order to stay pumped enough to get out of debt completely." In other words, the plan you choose doesn't matter if you don't stick with it.

Debt Avalanche vs. Debt Snowball: Which is the Best Way to Pay Off Debt?

So ... That brings us to our conclusion for this debate: I think you should have the best of both worlds. You should save as much time and money as possible *and* be rewarded, motivated, and congratulated every step of the way. Why choose between saving money, and feeling good about it?

5

Car Insurance Guide

A Car Insurance Guide to Help You Get What's Right for You

I don't know about you, but I've always found car insurance quite confusing—especially from a budget perspective. How do you save money while ensuring that you are legally protected? Staying legal on the road requires car insurance, whether you are driving a well-loved but time-worn set of wheels or an eye-popping show-room piece. Taking out a policy need not be painful in the wallet, however. Compared to home or life insurance, car insurance rates are influenced by factors that you have more control over.

Like cars, insurance policies are not created equal. You need to do a bit of digging to pull up the most attractive deals, and that starts with getting to know the insurance company. The top ones are covered in this guide, along with the kinds of insurance avail-able for car owners, versus the kind that fits their driving lifestyle, and some tips on how to save on your car insurance bill no matter which provider you choose.

Affordable Rates From The Best Auto Insurance Companies

Buying a new policy requires shopping around in the same man-ner that you would when buying a new vehicle, as there are sev-eral personal factors that influence your insurance premiums. To make the most of what's available in the insurance market, understand what each company offers at what cost to the cus-tomer. Discussed below are four car insurance companies that offer quality coverage at affordable rates. Match their offerings to your needs so you only pay for enough insurance that will get you sufficient coverage.

Choosing the best car insurance companies requires a set of criteria: 1) The company's ratings of financial strength as measured by A.M. Best; 2) Customer service satisfaction score as listed by J.D. Power; 3) The amount of information a customer has to give in order to receive a quote; 4) The ease and speed of getting a quote; 5) Available car insurance discounts; 6) Nationwide reach.

Using these criteria, the following insurance companies emerged at the top: Nationwide, State Farm, Travelers, and Progressive.

Nationwide – Cheap, No Frills Coverage

Using a dummy customer representing a female demographic of 40-year olds who drive older cars (like a 2006 Honda) in small Midwest cities, and who only want no-frills coverage enough to stay legal on the road, the top-ranking insurance company is Nationwide for its insurance coverage that meets the state minimum.

Using the dummy customer's information, her monthly auto insurance bill only costs less than $30, and exactly that amount if she adds coverage for underinsured and uninsured motorist liability. If she decides to get a $1,000 deductible for collision and comprehensive insurance, she'll only pay $21 more a month. She can also take advantage of Nationwide's 15 discounts to push her bill even lower.

Getting a quote from Nationwide doesn't require the customer to enter her Social Security number, only her phone number. The quote process is painless, taking only four minutes from start to end, and brings up minimum, standard and premium coverage options that can easily be customized.

As its name suggests, Nationwide has national reach. In terms of financial strength, A.M. Best gives it an outstanding A+ rating, while J.D. Power's annual survey ranks it at the lower half of the spectrum (with the exception for the north-central US) for customer satisfaction.

State Farm – One Of The Largest Auto Insurers

State Farm's quote process took about five minutes to complete, because it required more details such as the customer's SS number or driver's license number. Like Nationwide, customers can get three tiers of coverage that can be personalized.

State Farm bills the same dummy customer $63 for collision and comprehensive insurance with a $1,000 deductible, and only $5 more than Nationwide for coverage that meets the state minimum. At $35, the customer gets underinsured and uninsured motorist liability coverage. There are at least 12 published discounts for customers to take advantage of to further push down their bill.

State Farm maintains 18,000 agents across every state, making it one of the nation's largest car insurer. It also received stellar ratings from A.M. Best, getting A++ for financial strength, and obtained an above average rating in customer satisfaction according to J.D. Power.

Travelers – Stellar Financial Strength Rate

Getting top A++ marks from A.M. Best, Travelers auto insurance maintains 12,000 agents spread across the United States. New Yorkers are, in general, satisfied with the company's customer service, while insurance holders from other states think Travelers needs to work harder to improve its customer satisfaction ratings, according to the J.D. Power survey.

Travelers offers irresistible rates for the same dummy customer: only $3 more than Nationwide for state minimum coverage, and $3 on top of that for underinsured and uninsured motorist liability coverage. At the $1,000 deductible range, the same customer will only pay $74 for collision and comprehensive policy. The good news: cars with low mileage and drivers who took the defensive driving course may qualify for discounts, aside from the 12 others they can take advantage of.

Some information was pre-filled with the likeliest answers, so a customer won't need to enter her SSS to get a quote. Overall, the process was a breeze, barely going above three minutes to complete from beginning to end. There's also a "People Like You" feature that gives customers an idea on whether they are choosing coverage like people under the same circumstances as theirs.

Progressive – Discounts For Being A Good Student

The same customer would get a reasonable bill of $37 a month from Progressive to get coverage that meets the minimum for the state. Just like Travelers, Progressive requires only $3 more for underinsured and uninsured motorist liability coverage. An additional $48 gets the customer collision and comprehensive insurance with $1,000 deductibles. If you are a good student, a member of the military, or have several vehicles, you would qualify for even more discounts.

If you are looking for bundling benefits, you are likely going to get them from Progressive, which is fairly aggressive in marketing them. Otherwise, you can click, "No, thanks." The quote process was also quick and convenient, taking only three minutes to complete.

For those on a tight budget, they can put in their price and Progressive will pull up the coverage available at that price. Or they can choose to see coverage similar to what they already have, or get quotes by basic tiered levels. There's also a coverage checker to alert you if you are buying too little or too much insurance.

With more than 30,000 agents on its list, Progressive is undoubtedly all over the map. While J.D. Power customer satisfaction survey says it could do better in some states, it's in the middle of the rankings in the rest of the states. For financial strength, A.M. Best gives it an outstanding A+ rating.

Where To Get Auto Insurance Discounts

Getting affordable auto insurance rates means getting the most out of discounts, which many insurers offer in the form of bundled discounts for having multiple vehicles insured. Some discounts are not as apparent, so you need to dig deeper to get the best deals.

Driving Schools – Sign Up For A Defensive Driving Course

There is logic as to why adolescent drivers are cost-prohibitive to insure—they generally have little driving experience, they can be impulsive on the road, or they may engage in some other activities that could endanger their passengers or fellow drivers. These behaviors could lead to vehicular collisions, which for insurance companies translate to paying out claims. So if you are the kind of driver who takes every precaution to avoid car accidents by educating yourself about defensive driving, you are actually helping insurance companies save money.

A defensive driving class, which can be found through local community centers or your DMV, typically include traffic laws, inclement-weather driving, and alcohol- or drug-impaired driving, among other topics. These courses can be taken online or at a commercial driving school.

According to DriversEd.com, passing an accredited defensive driving course or any driver's ed class could mean up to a 10% discount. Some insurance companies may even waive insurance hikes on your premium (over a 12-month cycle) if you have recently received a ticket and enrolled in a defensive driving class.

To qualify for a discount, you need to present a certificate of completion. Some insurance companies may require you to have current certification or a retake of the course in order to continue receiving discounts. As classes are offered regularly and have flexible schedules, you can improve your driving skills anytime to continue saving money on car insurance premiums. You can even be eligible for steeper discounts if you've had all the drivers on your policy complete a defensive driving course.

Fifteen (15) states even require their drivers to complete a defensive driving education. These states are Illinois, Iowa, Kansas, Louisiana, Mississippi, Nebraska, Nevada, New Mexico, North Carolina, New Jersey, New York, Oklahoma, Oregon, Texas and Virginia.

"Good Student" Discounts – High Grades, Low Insurance Bill

Being a good student with high grades may earn you car insurance discounts. You need to be under 25, enrolled full-time at a high school, college or university, and maintain a GPA of at least 3.0 or be on the honor roll or dean's list to qualify. A letter signed by the school administrator or a current transcript has to be submitted as proof in order to obtain these discounts.

For students who are homeschooled, they need to obtain a desired percentile range (set forth by the insurance provider) from standardized test results and present their SAT or ACT scores in order to qualify. Sometimes, these discounts continue to be in effect for a limited time even after the student graduates.

Safe-Driver Discounts – Get Mileage Out Of A Clean Driving Record

Insurance companies make money when they don't settle car accident claims, so if you have a clean driving record, which is determined according to standards set by the insurance provider, you can bank on it and use it to avail yourself of significant discounts.

This makes a lot of business sense: by encouraging safe driving, car insurance companies maximize their revenues (from premiums and interest on these premiums they have invested) and minimize their payouts. Thus, they can pass on some of these benefits to those who are helping them save money.

While car insurance companies may define "safe driving" differently from one another, a clean driving record generally means you haven't been in collisions or accidents where you have been

found at fault. Safe driving also means avoiding moving violations such as driving under the influence, speeding, or reckless driving.

Resident Student Discounts – Get Coverage When You Are Home

For students attending college 100 miles away from home and returning home for vacations, resident student discounts may apply. The insured vehicle is often not used for driving on-campus, but instead used when the student is home.

Other discounts

Not all car insurance discounts are publicly available so you may need a bit of investigating when you're shopping around. For example, you may get lower rates if you automate your payments or pay your annual premium upfront. You could also get your premium lowered if you have installed car alarm systems or some other safety equipment. If you're in active military duty or a veteran, you may also get discounts specifically made for this market segment.

What Are The Major Types Of Auto Insurance?

Car insurance companies may have add-ons and other offerings, but all of those boil down to only three major types of auto insurance, namely:

Liability Coverage – Coverage For The Driver Not At Fault

Most states require liability coverage by law, which covers not the driver's own injuries or property damage but that of the other driver's personal injuries and property damage in a crash where the driver who took out the insurance is at fault.

The minimum amount of liability insurance, which remains the cheapest (though not the wisest option) for drivers, varies from state to state. In some cases, buying only liability coverage may be enough, while in others it may turn out to be much more expensive, as a bad crash could leave your other assets vulnerable.

While it's tempting to get only the barest minimum of coverage to keep your rates as low as possible, consider what it might cost you should you lack enough money for costs that are not covered by low state minimums.

Liability coverage could appear in your quote or car insurance policy in this format: 50/100/50. These numbers translate to $50,000 in bodily injury coverage for each person, $100,000 in total bodily injury coverage, and $50,000 in coverage for property damage. Minimum coverage amounts depend on each state.

Collision Coverage – Repair Or Replacement Cost

To pay for damage to your vehicle sustained in a crash where you are at fault, you need to buy collision coverage. This type of insurance may even cover costs in certain scenarios not covered under your other policies. Collision coverage may even pay in circumstances when another driver is at fault.

The amount your collision insurance will cover mostly depends on your car's value, although you control the deductible, which is the amount you pay out of pocket before the insurance company pays the rest.

Comprehensive Coverage – For All Other Car-Related Calamity

For any car-related calamity that your vehicle could run into over its life (minus the damage resulting from a crash), there's comprehensive car insurance for you, which is exactly what it says. Comprehensive insurance coverage is meant to complement collision coverage so in case of auto theft, damage from inclement weather or from a late-night collision with animals on the road, you'll be indemnified.

Because it's not meant to replace collision coverage, most drivers get comprehensive coverage to protect themselves and their vehicles against unforeseen accidents. You're still able to control the deductible, so the extra cost may turn out to save you money out of pocket.

Do I Really Need That Kind Of Car Insurance?

At first glance, buying comprehensive and collision coverage looks like a smarter choice. On paper, this would mean higher insurance premiums for you than when you buy liability-only coverage. For those who took out a loan to finance their vehicle purchase, there is little choice as to whether to get comprehensive and collision coverage—your lender will require proof. On the other hand, it's not wise to skip comprehensive and collision insurance if you don't have savings set aside for repairs or car-calamity expenses.

But if you use the car sparingly, you can opt to drop comprehensive and collision coverage. Or, if you drive an older vehicle that has been paid off and you are handy with car repair, or replacing the car in the event of damage is much cheaper, then carrying only liability coverage makes more financial sense. By way of example, if you drive a well-used 2004 Nissan Altima that has 150,000 miles on it, replacing it in case the car gets totaled will only set you back $2,000, an amount that you can easily put together if you have set aside an emergency fund.

If your vehicle is relatively new, say a 2011 Hyundai Sonata with only 12,000 miles on it, dropping the collision and comprehensive policies may mean higher out of pocket costs in case your car figures in a crash. You can take advantage of your clean driving record to get your rates lowered; paying 50% less on your insurance premium because you opted out of collision and coverage insurance will not let you save an amount enough for out-of-pocket car calamity costs. Paying $25 more a month will save you from incurring unexpected expenses should your car get totaled.

The takeaway lesson: The bare minimum to keep you legal on the road is liability coverage; it's also the most affordable car insurance. If replacing or repairing the car after a crash will mean major financial hardship, then taking out collision and comprehensive policies is more cost-effective.

Add-Ons And Other Kinds Of Coverage.

It's easy to pile on add-ons and jack up your insurance costs. But not all of them are created equal; you need to read the fine print to see if other types of insurance coverage or add-ons will benefit you and your vehicle. Of course, in states where such types of coverage are required, you have little choice but to pay up.

Before taking out a personal injury policy, which covers your medical expenses after a crash, go over your own health insurance plan to avoid overlap (which essentially boils down to getting the same coverage but paying twice as much).

However, you may have to buy uninsured or underinsured motorist coverage when driving in areas with a high percentage of uninsured drivers. This type of coverage pays for expenses that the (uninsured or underinsured) driver at fault cannot afford to pay. For only a few dollars more a month, paying for uninsured or underinsured motorist coverage is a decent bet.

Add-ons that pay for roadside assistance or rental cars while your car is under repair may not be as smart an investment. Your AAA membership may even offer a better deal if and when you need roadside assistance, and borrowing a car from a friend or covering the cost of a rental car may render rental car riders too expensive.

What Car Insurance Should I Get In My State?

Depending on where you live, you may or may not need more than liability insurance (which pays for bodily injury and property damage), which is the bare minimum to keep you legal on the road. Some states however go a bit further, requiring other riders such as personal injury protection and uninsured or underinsured motorist coverage.

To find out whether you need more than just liability coverage (and how much), you can go to the Insurance Information Institute for details. As of September 2015, New Hampshire is the only state that does not require liability insurance, but mandates that the driver at fault should have enough funds to meet state requirements in the event of a crash.

Find Affordable Car Insurance With These Six Tips.

Hunting for good bargains requires a bit of legwork, and finding the right kind of car insurance at the most affordable price is no different. Of course, there are factors such as your age, gender, marital status, job and location that are beyond your control, but affect your car insurance rates to a large degree.

Other factors, however, are well within your reach to change. These are the kind of car you drive and how you drive it. Take advantage of these factors under your control and make them work for you to find the cheapest car insurance that will provide sufficient coverage. Comparison shop and take advantage of discounts and bundling offers to drive down your insurance costs. Here's how.

Compare Costs And Benefits

Shopping around these days doesn't mean making endless phone calls or filling out forms on dozens of websites. Just like airfare aggregators, online quote tools give you an idea—at a glance—of how much you're likely to pay when buying from several auto insurance companies.

There are many factors that affect your rate, so what was quoted for a friend or another member of the family may not be the same amount quoted for you. You have to compare apples to apples, and an online quote tool allows you to do this.

Take Advantage Of Bundling Discounts

If you already have life or home policies from a certain provider, it may be more convenient to go with that company for your auto insurance needs. You can bundle policies and get cheaper rates in return.

Of course, bundling coverage doesn't always translate to savings. Dedicated auto insurance companies sometimes offer irresistible discounts to keep their customers from switching. This could translate to cheaper car insurance if you keep policies with different insurers.

Increase Your Deductible

Generally, a plan with a lower deductible would cost more than a plan with a higher deductible. Deductibles are what you pay out of pocket before your insurance pays for the rest of the cost to replace or repair your vehicle.

As an example, a $100 deductible on comprehensive and collision coverage requires a premium of $120 a month. This is on a policy for a female in her early thirties with a clean driving record living in a small southern city and using a 2011 Hyundai Sonata that averages 12,000 miles a year. Raising that deductible by $150 decreased the insurance bill by $20, which means a savings of $240 a year. Going as high as $1000 for a deductible brings down the monthly insurance bill to only $82, a savings of $456 (12 months x $38) a year on car insurance alone.

Of course, this suggests that you had set aside $1,000 for just this purpose. Otherwise, increasing your deductible and decreasing your monthly car insurance bill would make more sense. As a rule, the cleaner your driving record and the less of a risk you pose to the insurance company, the lower your insurance bill will be.

Drive A Sensible Car.

High-powered or luxury rides are always the most expensive to insure because they are magnets for theft, cost a lot more to fix or replace, and tend to get their drivers into more trouble—situations that could cost the insurance company a handsome settlement claim and which understandably, it would want to avoid.

Take for instance the 600-horsepower Nissan GT-R Nismo, which was the most expensive 2015 car to insure: its owner pays $3,574 a year in car insurance, according to Insure.com. Other powerful sporty luxury cars that top the $3,000 a year insurance bill are Porsche 911, Carrera S Cabriolet, Mercedes-Benz SL65 AMG Convertible, Audi R8 5.2 Spyder Quattro, and Dodge SRT Viper.

Cars that were easy on the wallet to purchase are similarly easy on the wallet to insure. Their drivers tend to be more careful on the road, the repair or replacement cost is not as expensive and the cars are not as attractive to thieves. Examples are minivans, smaller SUVs, and sedans.

The cheapest vehicle that cost the least to insure is the Jeep Wrangler Sport, which only requires about $1,134 a year in premiums. Other vehicles that are cheap to insure are Honda CR-V LX, Dodge Journey SXT, Jeep Patriot Sport, Honda CR-V LX, and Honda Odyssey EX-L. They may be less glamorous rides, but they get you from A to B (if that is all you need) and don't cost an arm and a leg to maintain and to insure.

Improve Your Driving Behavior.

Every time you take out a policy, your car insurance company bets that you won't total the car so they won't have to make a massive payout. Any driving behavior that increases your risk of getting into a vehicular collision or any other type of car calamity, such as getting a driving ticket regularly or getting caught driving under the influence jacks up your insurance bill. To keep your premium low, maintain a clean driving record, which can take time to achieve if you began with a spotty one.

Some other insurance saving tips are not as obvious: There's virtue in driving less. Not only will you decrease your carbon footprint and your gas expense, you will also decrease your auto insurance premium. The reason: less time behind the wheel equals a lower chance of filing a claim. If you've gone the way of carpooling or taking the subway, be sure to tell your insurance provider so your insurance bill can get adjusted.

Keep Your Credit In Top Shape.

To lower your monthly insurance bill, keep not just a clean driving record, but also an exemplary credit standing. Your credit report speaks volumes not just of your spending habits, but also of your driving habits, according to insurers. It may not seem fair, but insurers assume that those who have good credit are statistically less likely to file a claim than those with lower credit scores. If your credit score is at the bottom of the pile, expect to pay as much as four times more than someone with a spotless credit history.

If your credit score can benefit from some improvement, you may want to move to California, Maryland, Hawaii and Massachusetts, where this controversial practice is illegal. Otherwise, you will need to put in the hard work to improve your credit score in an attempt to decrease your insurance bill.

Remember to re-evaluate your car insurance annually, or as often as your circumstances change, meaning anything that would affect your driving habit and your risk of getting into road trouble. Keep your eyes peeled for good old-fashioned competition that always has the potential to attract and keep customers with cheap car insurance policies.

Student Loans

Worried About Student Loan Debt? Here Are 15 Ways To Help You Deal With It

College education can be a tough financial burden, if the $1.2 trillion student loan crisis is any indication. It's no wonder then that many graduates start out with $40,000 in student loans, and even upwards of $50,000 (for 19% of borrowers) if they continued with higher degrees or changed majors, according to the Federal Reserve Board Survey of Consumer Finances. In fact, according to the same source, some 5.6% of students owe over $100,000.

Wiping The Slate Clean – Getting Out Of Student Loan Debt

It's easy to get disheartened when you are facing seemingly insur-mountable debt before you even began hunting for a job that will get you in the black. While college debt repayment can seem like an impossible mountain to conquer, paying off every cent of student loan you accrued in college can be done with a bit of planning and plenty of grit. Here are some of the ways to get the student loan repayment ball rolling.

Make Your Grace Period Work For You

It's easy to fall into the grace period trap, but don't. Get a head start with your six-month grace period by understanding your loans, drawing up a repayment plan, and paying down your loan anyway, even if you just start with the minimum amount. You will have been used to not missing your monthly payments once the actual payment begins. Not all student loans qualify for this grace period, so find out if yours does, and explore alternatives if it doesn't.

Learn As Much As You Can About Your Loans

As with anything in life, knowing your loans is winning half the battle, as not all loans are created equal. There might be some hidden perks you ought to know to make the most impact on your student loan debt, and knowing these perks require some investigation. Here's how.

Step 1: Track Down Your Loans

Between burying your nose in your studies, working part-time to help fund your tuition, and enjoying college life, it's easy to lose track of all the loans you took out. If you can't remember how much you owe whom, you can look it up using the National Student Loan Data System to check if you have any federal loans. You can also order a free copy of your credit report to whomever else you need to repay and maybe contact these private lenders directly.

Step 2: Explore Your Payment Options

You may not be in a position right now to make your minimum monthly payments, or any payment at all, so you might want to apply for a temporary deferment. Or you can find out which of your loans allow you to change to a payment plan based on how much you earn at the moment.

Step 3: Know As Much As You Can About Each Loan's Details

It's not unusual for college students to be dealing with multiple loans. Your first task is to identify which of these loans charge you the highest interest so you can first tackle that before the lower interest loans. You also need to know the minimum payments you need to make each month, and which of these loans would qualify you for loan forgiveness, deferment, or at least a better payment plan.

Select The Payment Plan Best Suited To Your Current Situation

Pay-as-you-earn or income-based repayment are just some of the options available for you if you need to work around your current income. If keeping track of multiple loans makes your head ache, you may want to consider student loan consolidation.

Don't Leave the "College Lifestyle" Just Yet

Understandably, you may want to have a break after four years of burning the midnight oil and feasting on ramen noodles. You may feel that after all those years of hard work and sleep deprivation you finally deserve to splurge. Hold off on that temptation for now and buckle down on debt repayment. Only by facing the reality of your debt situation and gritting your teeth to fulfil your financial obligations will you be able to get out student loan debt faster. Otherwise, you will be in a more vulnerable position if in the near future you lose your current job and you are nowhere near your repayment goals.

Remember, there are plenty of ways to live a frugal lifestyle and still not feel deprived. After all, you survived college and still had fun, didn't you? So continue clipping coupons, hunting down bargains, and cooking at home for now to get your expenses within bounds. Find a roommate you can split your rent with, take advantage of free exhibits in museums and galleries, walk and bike whenever possible, carpool with friends, and take public transportation. In place of expensive concert tickets and fancy meals and drinks, get together with family and friends for a potluck dinner or weekend camping.

Create A Budget And Stick To It

Having a zero-based budget is crucial when you are trying to reduce debt, because it compels you to look hard at your spending habits and forces you to trim where it doesn't hurt. Then put it down in black and white and follow the plan. Explore creative ways to save money and put that savings toward student loan debt repayment.

Draw Up A Savvy Debt Repayment Plan

As if student loans were not enough of a burden to start with, college graduates sometimes have to pay off credit card debt to the tune of $3,200. That's the average figure, but it could be a lot higher according to Debt.org. It's easy to get wrapped up in repaying your student loan first, but don't overlook your plastic; missing monthly payments there will show up on your credit report. Understand how much you're paying in interest every month, and figure out how to deal with it moving forward.

Pursue Varied Or Better Income Streams

Sometimes, no matter how you scrimp, you just can't make ends meet, in which case it may be high time for you to find new sources of income. Is it possible to get a part-time job near your present workplace or home so you can easily stitch them together? Do you love shopping? Turn the table around and sell your unwanted belongings online, at a yard sale, or to consignment shops. Do you love to play guitar in your spare time? You may be good enough to put up a shingle for music tutorials online or in person. In short, monetize the things that you love doing for free anyway. If you're currently employed, consider asking for a raise. Evaluate how else you can contribute to your workplace and see if you can get extra shifts or apply to a higher paying job.

Deduct Your Student Loan Interest From Your Taxable Income

It may not amount to much, but remember, you are entitled to claim student loan interest as a deductible expense from your taxable income, which could amount to as much as $2,500. Check with your lender for interest you've paid for the tax year, so you'll have that figure on hand once tax season rolls around.

Consider Loan Forgiveness

Rural areas or low income neighborhoods routinely lack specific professions, which are often the most needed, such as teachers, doctors, lawyers, law enforcement officers, firefighters, dentists, nurses, social workers and psychiatrists, to name a few. In exchange for your services in these areas, you may qualify for loan forgiveness. Depending on the degree you earned or the industry you are currently working in, you can take advantage of the loan forgiveness program as long as you are willing to stick to stipulations.

Some of the contracts may require you to render a number of hours of work or a number of months to live in the area. Otherwise, you may have to return part of the student loan assistance you received, or not get assistance at all if you don't complete your contract.

Sign Up With Volunteer Organizations

If you love helping people, make it work for you by signing up with volunteer organizations. Some of these are VISTA (Volunteers In Service to America), AmeriCorps, Teach for America, Peace Corps, the National Health Service Corps, along with newcomers Zerobound and SponsorChange. In exchange, these organizations may offer loan forgiveness or reimburse you for your service. The latter two specifically connect you to organizations that need volunteers in exchange for money towards your student loan debt.

In the same way that you sign a contract with loan forgiveness providers, you will also fulfill certain requirements to satisfy these contracts, which you should understand very carefully before signing on. Depending on the program, only some loans may qualify.

Move To A Place With A Lower Cost Of Living

Take advantage of differing costs of living from around the country. To attract young, educated professionals, some cities entice this crowd by offering some type of relocation incentive. Some examples are Detroit, Michigan; Niagara Falls, New York; and Saskatchewan, Canada. As with any other loan forgiveness program, there are stipulations that you need to adhere to, some of which might require you to live in a designated area or work for a specific company for a certain period.

Even if you don't move for reasons of getting reimbursed for your student debts, you may want to consider moving anyway to keep your cost of living low. If you prefer not to be tied down with contracts, you may want to find a closer place to move to where you can get cheaper rent or where work is within walking distance. That way, you won't have to worry about car payments, maintenance, insurance, gas, parking tolls, registration renewals and other incidental costs of owning a car. If you don't need to show up to work physically, you are definitely in a better position to move to an area with lower cost of living and an environment more suited to your lifestyle and goals. Then you can channel your savings to student loan debt repayment.

Enroll Your Accounts In Auto Debit

You won't miss money you didn't have in the first place, so take advantage of an auto-debit program before you spend the money somewhere unproductive. You may even quality for a twenty-five percent reduction off the interest of your loan if you sign up for auto debit with Sallie Mae. The amount is not something that will wipe out your college loans overnight, but they do add up quite nicely over time. On top of that, you avoid the possibility of paying penalties for late or missed payments, which can hit you twice— higher interest expense, and a mark on your credit report.

Continue Paying Interest During Deferment

Deferment is meant to give you breathing room when money is tight, like when you are unemployed, in school, or facing an economic hardship. You may even get deferment when you are an active military member. But even if you have a situation approved for deferment, continue sending interest payments in your loan to ease the burden once your deferment is up.

Sign Up With Upromise

If you love buying online anyway, Upromise, considered one of the Best Credit Cards for students, will let you earn check back or cash back up to five percent. Set up an account, enroll all your credit cards and loyalty cards, and let these financial tools work for you. Even better, you can let your family and friends help you out by sharing the link with them and encouraging them to use it so the credit counts toward your account. You may even link this perk to any Sallie Mae student loan you have, or enjoy a check back.

Delay Taking On Big Debts Right After College

Getting started after graduation can be expensive, and it's tempting to tack on more debt before you have cleared your student loans. You need to plan carefully for goals after graduation. Can you really afford a car or a house of your own? Riding public transportation and renting may prove to be cheaper in the long run, at least until you have paid off all of your college debt.

When it's time to settle down, ask yourself if you want to work years more for an event that happened only for a day. The average wedding cost can easily set you back $30,000, and even higher if you live in a large city or if you're planning an extravagant affair. While you may feel that you deserve to have that special day celebrated with no expense spared, digging yourself deeper into debt is not a wise financial move when you are starting a family. Instead, consider a less traditional and more affordable wedding which may prove to be even more memorable and meaningful, not just for you but for your spouse too.

7

Personal Finance Blogs

Personal Finance Blogs

Blog	Website
Afford Anything	AffordAnything.com
Budgets Are Sexy	BudgetsAreSexy.com
Mr. Money Mustache	MrMoneyMustache.com
I Will Teach You To Be Rich	IWillTeachYouToBeRich.com
Money After Graduation	MoneyAfterGraduation.com
Blonde on a Budget	BlondeonaBudget.com
The Simple Dollar	TheSimpleDollar.com
Frugalwoods	Frugalwoods.com
Len Penzo	LenPenzo.com
Frugaling	Frugaling.org
Financial Samurai	FinancialSamurai.com
The Penny Hoarder	ThePennyHoarder.com
Life and My Finances	LifeAndMyFinances.com

8

Top 25 Social Influencers in Personal Finance and Wealth

2016's Top 25 Social Influencers In Personal Finance & Wealth

MoneyTips2016's Top 25Social Influencers in Personal Finance & Wealth. Each of these professionals leverages social media to the fullest in order to help their audience make wise investments, manage assets in an effective manner, and start down the road to financial freedom. Congratulations to everyone who made the list!

- Dave Ramsey, @DaveRamsey – American Financial Author; Host, *The Dave Ramsey Show*; Founder, Ramsey Solutions
- Robert T. Kiyosaki, @theRealKiyosaki – Financial Education Advocate; Founder & Author, The Rich Dad Company
- Suze Orman, CFP, @SuzeOrmanShow – Host, *The Suze Orman Show* and *Suze Orman's Financial Essentials*; Contributing Finance Editor, *O, The Oprah Magazine*
- Josh Brown, @ReformedBroker – CEO, Ritholtz Wealth Management; Contributor CNBC's *Fast Money/Halftime Report*
- Clark Howard, @ClarkHoward – Host, *The Clark Howard Show*; *New York Times* #1 best-selling author
- Alan Krueger, @Alan_Krueger – Professor of Economics, Princeton University
- Mr. Money Mustache, @mrmoneymustache – Founder & Blogger, MrMoneyMustache.com
- Jason Zweig, @JasonZweigWSJ – Investing columnist for *The Wall Street Journal*; author of*Your Money and Your Brain*
- Barry Ritholtz, @ritholtz – Founder & Chief Investment Officer, Ritholtz Wealth Management
- Todd Duncan, @toddstweets – CEO/Founder, The Duncan Group
- Lauren Young, @LaurenYoung – Money editor, *Thomson Reuters*

- Charles Passy, @CharlesPassy – Staff Writer, *Dow Jones*; previously held roles at MarketWatch.com, SmartMoney.com, *SmartMoney Magazine*, and other financial publications
- Blake Ellis, @blakeellis3 – Investigative writer, CNNMoney.com
- Carl Richards, CFP, @behaviorgap – Director of Investor Education, BAM Advisor Services; Columnist, *The New York Times*
- Zain Asher, @ZainAsher – International anchor, CNN; former CNN business correspondent and reporter for CNNMoney.com
- Jose Pagliery, @Jose_Pagliery – Cybersecurity reporter, CNNMoney.com; author of *Bitcoin and the Future of Money*
- Michelle Singletary, @SingletaryM – Personal Finance Columnist, *The Washington Post*
- Ben Carlson, CFA, @awealthofcs – Director of Institutional Asset Management, Ritholtz Wealth Management; author of *A Wealth of Common Sense*
- Jean Chatzky, @JeanChatzky – Financial Editor, NBC's *TODAY Show*; Columnist & Financial Ambassador, AARP
- Tara Siegel Bernard, @tarasbernard – Personal Finance & Consumer Reporter, *The New York Times*
- Karen Damato, @DamatoK – Wealth editor, *The Wall Street Journal*
- Jesse Eisinger, @eisingerj – Senior reporter, *ProPublica*; former Wall Street Editor, Conde Nast
- Ron Lieber, @ronlieber – *Your Money* columnist, *New York Times*; author of *The Opposite of Spoiled: Raising Kids Who Are Grounded, Generous, and Smart About Money*
- Tracy Shannon Levey, @TaxAddict – Co-Founder & VP of Communications, Parker Tax Publishing
- Natali Morris, @natalimorris – News anchor, MSNBC; contributor, CNBC and the *TODAY Show*; Creator, natalimorris.com

Personal Finance Books

Personal Finance Books

The Millionaire Next Door: The Surprising Secrets of America's Wealthy
Thomas J. Stanley & William D. Danko

Most of the truly wealthy in this country don't live in Beverly Hills or on Park Avenue—they live next door. This bestselling book identifies seven common traits that show up again and again among those who have accumulated wealth.

I Will Teach You To Be Rich
Ramit Sethi

A six-week personal finance program for 20-to-35-year-olds based on the four pillars of personal finance: banking, saving, budgeting, and investing. Along with the wealth building ideas of personal entrepreneurship.

The Automatic Millionaire: A Powerful One-Step Plan To Live & Finish Rich
David Bach

A realistic system, based on timeless principles, with everything you need to know, including phone numbers and websites, so you can put the secret to becoming an Automatic Millionaire in place from the comfort of your own home. You don't need a budget, you don't need willpower, you don't need to make a lot of money, you don't need to be that interested in money, and you can set up the plan in an hour.

The Richest Man in Babylon
George S. Clason

Beloved by millions, this timeless classic hails as one the greatest inspirational works on the subject of thrift, financial planning, and personal wealth. These fascinating and informative stories set you on a sure path to prosperity and its accompanying joys.

The Total Money Makeover: A Proven Plan for Financial Fitness
Dave Ramsey

This is the simplest, most straightforward game plan for completely making over your money habits based on results. This book will help you: design a sure-fire plan for paying off all debt—cars, houses, everything—recognize the 10 most dangerous money myths, and secure a big, fat nest egg for emergencies and retirement!

Think and Grow Rich
Napoleon Hill

Published in 1937, Hill draws on stories of Andrew Carnegie, Thomas Edison, Henry Ford, and other millionaires of his generation to illustrate his principles. In the updated version, Arthur R. Pell, Ph.D. deftly interweaves anecdotes of how contemporary millionaires and billionaires, such as Bill Gates, Mary Kay Ash, Dave Thomas, and Sir John Templeton, achieved their wealth.

Rich Dad Poor Dad: What The Rich Teach Their Kids About Money That the Poor and Middle Class Do Not!
Robert T. Kiyosaki

Rich Dad Poor Dad, the #1 Personal Finance book of all time, tells the story of Robert Kiyosaki and his two dads—his real father and the father of his best friend, his rich dad—and the ways in which both men shaped his thoughts about money and investing. The book explodes the myth that you need to earn a high income to be rich and explains the difference between working for money and having your money work for you.

The Money Book for the Young, Fabulous & Broke
Suze Orman

The world's most trusted expert on money matters answers a generation's cry for help and gives advice on: credit card debt, student loans, credit scores, the first real job, buying a first home, insurance facts (auto, home, renters, and health), financial issues of the self-employed, and much more that fits the realities of "Generation Broke."

10

Personal Finance Vision Board

Creating a Financial Vision Board

If you're anything like me, it helps to see your goals crystalized in black and white. A vision board is an easy and inexpensive way to crystalize your goals.

What is a vision board you ask? Basically, it's a poster or bulletin board filled with images and words that illustrate your ideal life. You can tear photos from magazines, put up cards, print Google images, or draw whatever it is you need. The benefits of this exercise are twofold: not only can mapping out your priorities help you determine where your money should go, tapping into your deepest desires can set you on a path to achieving what may seem out of reach today.

The simple act of seeing your goals goes a long way toward helping you focus your energy on making your goals a reality.

A vision board is a powerful visualization tool that you can use as inspiration for the journey toward your ideal life. Some people refer to it as a "dream board" or an "inspiration board." No matter what you call it, it's basically a collage of pictures, words and quotes that serve to remind you of your passion and purpose.

You don't have to be an artist to make a vision board! All you need are a few basic supplies and instructions to get started.

You'll need:

- Poster board, cork board or a small canvas
- A stack of old magazines
- Scissors
- Markers or paint
- Glue, tape, thumbtacks or pin

- A photo of yourself

Now, let's get started.

Set aside about an hour to complete your vision board. Go to a quiet space in your home where you can concentrate on yourself for a little while.

- Create a relaxing atmosphere. Play some inspiring music. Light some candles. Close your eyes and take a moment to reflect on your big goals and dreams. What do you want your ideal financial life to look like?
- Cut out images from magazines that represent the life you want to live. If you are including specific goals in your vision board, it's important that you spend some time discovering how you will accomplish them. You want to make sure your goals are: specific, measurable, attainable, realistic and timely. You also want to make sure your vision board is inspiring and fun to look at—remember, you will be reflecting on it daily!
- Place a photo of yourself in the middle of the board. Then paste or pin your magazine images on your board. There's no "right way" to arrange your images. You can fill the board with pictures, or just have a few posted all over on the board.
- Use your markers or paint to write your personal financial mission statement or other quotes on your vision board. You can also just cut out words or phrases from the magazines to paste on your board that remind you of the life you want to live.

Display your vision board somewhere you'll see it every day and feel inspired! If you like, you can also frame your vision board and hang it on your wall.

And there you have it. An easy, step-by-step process for creating a financial vision board to help you reach your goals.

Conclusion

While I dedicated this book to my Aunt Ellen and Miss Barbara Kent, I would be remiss if I did not also acknowledge my father, James Willie.

During the "heat of the moment," as often happens between mothers and daughters, my mother would always tell me that I was "my father's daughter." I trust that wasn't intended to be a compliment. I was stubborn. I was singularly focused. I viewed life in black and white with no room for gray. The list was a pretty long list. However, when it came to personal finance, I wore my likeness to my Daddy like a badge of honor.

My father was a quiet man. He did not talk much, but when he did speak, watch out! Using my "Grandma skills," the lessons that I learned from him were learned by observing the way he managed his financial life, not by sharing "quality time." He was busy working—sometimes three jobs at a time.

Before becoming a longshoreman—a job he held for 33 years—he hustled by painting/paneling apartments and by fixing cars. Both he and my Mother, a registered psychiatric nurse, did what they needed to do to put food on the table and keep a roof over our heads.

James Willie was the only person that I know of who purchased a new car every two years. Cash. We're not talking a Volkswagen Rabbit (my first car), we're talking a BMW, Mercedes or a Volvo. During my youth, James paid cash for all three of the childhood homes I lived in.

When he transitioned in 2004, his only debt was the annual membership fee for his American Express Platinum card. He did not believe in debt. He believed in hard work and in sacrifice. He did not believe in living beyond his means. He believed in saving.

My father's financial legacy can best be captured by the quote that I selected for my high school profile, "Mama may have, and Papa may have. But, God bless the child that's got his own."

Again, while I did not spend a lot of "quality time" with my father, I learned by observing the way he lived his financial life. His example allowed me to be open to receiving the financial lessons of Miss Kent.

Thank you, James Willie. With love your "hard-headed" (I preferred the nickname "Grandma") daughter, Marian.

NOTES

NOTES

NOTES

NOTES

NOTES

NOTES

NOTES

NOTES

NOTES